David Stavanger is a poet, performer, editor, cultural producer and lapsed psychologist. In 2013 he won the Arts Queensland Thomas Shapcott Poetry Prize for *The Special* (UQP), which was awarded the 2015 Wesley Michel Wright Poetry Prize. He was co-director of the Queensland Poetry Festival from 2015 to 2017, and has been at the forefront of founding poetry slam in Australia. Also known as the Green Room-nominated spoken word artist Ghostboy, he lives between the stage and the page.

Anne-Marie Te Whiu is a cultural producer and editor. She was co-director of the Queensland Poetry Festival from 2015 to 2017, and is co-editor of *Verity La*'s spoken word stream 'Slot Machine' and 'Discoursing Diaspora'. Anne-Marie is an emerging Māori-Australian poet, weaver and experienced theatre practitioner, having studied a Double Major in Drama and Literature and winning several short play awards as a director. Born and raised in Brisbane, she is a proud descendant of the Te Rarawa tribe in Northland, Aotearoa.

SOLID AIR

AUSTRALIAN AND NEW ZEALAND SPOKEN WORD

EDITED BY
DAVID STAVANGER
& ANNE-MARIE TE WHIU

UQP

First published 2019 by University of Queensland Press
PO Box 6042, St Lucia, Queensland 4067 Australia

uqp.com.au
uqp@uqp.uq.edu.au

Illustrations (cover and page v) by Des Skordilis (Skords)
Cover design by Design by Committee (Josh Durham)
Typeset in 11.25/14 pt Adobe Garamond Pro by Post Pre-press Group, Brisbane
Printed in Australia by McPherson's Printing Group

Australian Government | Australia Council for the Arts | ARTS COUNCIL OF NEW ZEALAND TOI AOTEAROA

This project has been assisted by the Australian Government through the Australia Council, its arts
funding and advisory body, and the support of Creative New Zealand Toi Aotearoa.

A catalogue record for this book is available from the National Library of Australia.

ISBN 978 0 7022 6259 3 (pbk)
ISBN 978 0 7022 6372 9 (pdf)
ISBN 978 0 7022 6373 6 (epub)
ISBN 978 0 7022 6374 3 (kindle)

MIX
Paper from
responsible sources
FSC® C001695

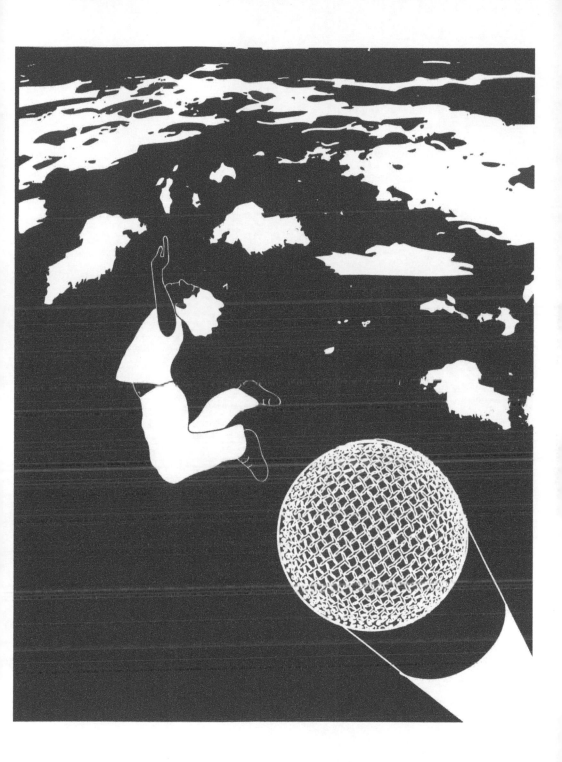

Contents

Foreword
ALISON WHITTAKER

Have you ever held your breath? Of course you have. Try doing it again with me.

Rocks form in your lungs and fill your chest. You become aware of air – sometimes by its lack and sometimes by its taste and sometimes by its movement and sometimes by drawing it in, shuddering and spluttering. Air is present, but by our taking account of it, it can become solid. Our desire for breath gnaws against the overwhelming pressure of air until we give in to it. Within a few minutes, we forget air again – but it is worth doing the exercise if only to make real our reliance on it.

When I was younger I would hold my breath in cars to measure streets. While I did, men talked on the radio about how the drought was making the chicken hawks hunt puppies, but they also gave away cash prizes where women called in and screamed with joy. Sound travels through matter – through the radio speakers to me – but voices came to our car, our little can of solid air in which I tried not to breathe, through radio waves at 92.9 MHz. When they fell silent it was called 'dead air' and everyone in the car would turn to look at the radio, as if for the first time noticing it. Or we'd tune in to the scanner and wait to hear what the cops and truckies were doing. It's an instinct replicated again and again at performance poetry events, or in poetic multimedia in a digital space. The poet gulps in nervousness and our eyes move to the mic. They thumb for the page, or look into the middle distance, to remember their next spit. Maybe a host or techie rushes in to help. The air dies, or is taken away, and we are rapt.

Co-editors David Stavanger and Anne-Marie Te Whiu are alchemists in pressing *Solid Air* to our lips. Not because it's any real feat to remember air, but because it's an achievement to curate a sense that air is solid without first taking anything away. Rather than depriving us of air, *Solid Air* gives it to us in abundance. It faces down the challenge of curating spoken poetry, an ephemeral art form that is without doubt experiencing a resurgence throughout Australia and New Zealand worth documenting. It creates a little record of the moment when a poet reworks the air around them – before our breath calms down and we forget air again.

Solid Air is an important and timely anthology that brings together the excellence, passion and compassion of a wide variety of voices with a transformative vision for what poetry is and does; who it mobilises and how, who it represents and how, who it nurtures and how, and who it targets and how. Credit goes to the book's editors, David and Anne-Marie, both poets who have made a world in which other poets flourish. Like air, this collection adapts to atmospheric changes without neglecting something fundamental; how poetry is about negotiating power as much as rearranging air. This negotiation is present as it moves from face-to-face and broadcast performance to the more static, secluded page.

Solid Air lingers like a conversation. This book is so ambitious, so large, so very expansive, conveying something I can barely overhear. And there's no dead air. Only something solid – and now it's in your hands.

Introduction
DAVID STAVANGER AND ANNE-MARIE TE WHIU

> 'Language lives when you speak it. Let it be heard. The worst thing that can happen to words is that they go unsaid.' — Kate Tempest

Solid Air attempts to physicalise what spoken word poetry is (and can be) – that which one is compelled to speak / that which one cannot hold silent. Spoken word is more than hard-earned memorisation or performance technique. It is a lived and living thing: within the skin of the text, the song of the line, the architecture of sound. Performance poetry is on one level ephemeral but that doesn't mean the writing can't endure beyond the moment. On these pages sit words that have often first been performed in a live context to an audience. The pulse of those moments still hangs between the lines.

Over the past decade, spoken word has become a central part – if not the beating heart – of contemporary Australian and New Zealand poetry. Since the Australian Poetry Slam developed into a truly national competition in 2008, followed by its close cousin the New Zealand National Slam in 2011, a range of distinct voices have emerged. These poets draw on a combination of US slam culture (which predominantly came out of the Chicago scene and New York's Nuyorican Poetry Café); Australian experimental performance poetry subculture; the growing influence of hip hop; modern protest and social movements; and intergenerational oral storytelling traditions led by Indigenous peoples from both lands.

During this time the Australian Poetry Slam, founded by Miles Merrill, and the collective-run New Zealand Poetry Slam have become outward faces of the form, elevating poetry into the public consciousness. This period has seen the establishment of key spoken word organisations and regular local poetry slams held across both countries, building on years of previous grassroots development.

Many major writers festivals have moved away from the outdated notion that a poet must have published a book to be booked, increasingly building performative writers into their line-ups. *Solid Air* is a living survey of the contemporary spoken word landscape from 2008 to 2018, a fertile period when spoken word lay down new roots across the region, as both a serious art form in its own right *and* as a poetry that warrants being taken seriously.

'It's important that marginalised voices are given as much space (if not more) than the dominant voices we hear so much from.'
— Candy Royalle

The term 'spoken word' has allowed a generation of writers – often young, diverse and politically active – the freedom to establish a new poetic that addresses the world within and around them directly in terms they can claim as their own. It has led to an increased democratisation of the form, with people from a broad range of backgrounds finding a platform that encourages all voices to access and create poetry. This can be seen in the joyous rise of Bankstown Poetry Slam, currently Australia's largest spoken word event, and the groundbreaking South Auckland Poets' Collective. In 2013 Te Kahu Rolleston became the first Māori artist to take out the NZ Poetry Slam. In 2018 Melanie Mununggurr-Williams became the first Indigenous Australian poetry slam champion, and in the same year the Māori youth spoken word collective Ngā Hinepūkōrero won New Zealand's WORD The Frontline Grand Slam. These are all defining moments in terms of who spoken word can elevate, celebrate and mobilise.

This is one of the most beautiful aspects of spoken word – it is a room where there's room for everyone. Central to the ecology of spoken word is the artist returning back to community. Established names often forfeit fees to feature at regular gigs to keep growing the form, continuing connection and providing aspiration for emerging voices to pursue spoken word beyond their two minutes. Once in front of the mic, any artist can be as significant as another.

'These are the forthcoming generations and for me that's about connecting with the present and not thinking of poetry as a museum.'
— Simon Armitage, UK Poet Laureate, *The Telegraph* 2015

While the art form has predominantly been characterised as a popular live performative art, it is undeniable that in recent years spoken word has established itself as an important and valid written form overseas, helping to turn around both poetry's flagging popularity and book sales, despite elements of establishment pushback. The appearance of Button Poetry in 2011, the first YouTube channel dedicated to spoken word, has filled the void left by Def Jam Poetry, creating some of the first viral online poems. In the US, World Poetry Slam finalist Danez Smith became the youngest recipient of the Forward Prize for his 2017 collection *Don't Call Us Dead*, which also went on to become a finalist for the US National Book Award. While in the UK, the likes of Hollie McNish and Kate Tempest (who have respectively won the Ted Hughes and T.S. Eliot Prizes and are currently amongst the UK's best-selling poets) illustrate the growing appetite for spoken word. That Warsan Shire's poetry features on Beyoncé's *Lemonade* album confirms this trend.

The success of these artists demonstrates the role spoken word has played – alongside the emergence of the Instagram poets – in redefining contemporary poetry. Local leading practitioners such as Omar Musa, Maxine Beneba Clarke, Luka Lesson, Hera Lindsay Bird, Selina Tusitala Marsh, Courtney Sina Meredith and Candy Royalle have been at the forefront of this paradigm shift, becoming some of the best-known and most dynamic poets today, with work that transcends both the page and the stage.

'There is a spectre haunting Australian poetry – it is the spectre of spoken word.' — Ali Alizadeh, *Cordite* 2005

Despite generational shifts and a few breaking through, it seems that the ghost is still in the building. Spoken word artists and performance-based poets have been noticeably absent in print across our region, especially in major poetry journals and anthologies such as the *Best Australian Poems* series. Similarly, *Best New Zealand Poems'* main criteria is to select only previously published work. Renowned Australian poet/anarchist Π.O., wrote a review of *Contemporary Australian Poetry* (2016) in *Southerly* (77.1, 2017), observing this limited scope and noting the lack of spoken word included in the collection even though the four editors 'acknowledge that many changes had occurred in the poetry scene during the period 1990 to 2016 (the period covered by the anthology) and that those changes "occurred off the page".'

Literary magazines such as *Catalyst* (Christchurch) and *Going Down Swinging* (Melbourne) are two exceptions to this rule, and this has been backed in more recent times by the *Australian Poetry Journal's 8.2 Spoken* edition, which was the first time a mainstream poetry journal showcased spoken word on the page. This lack of representation – and at times erasure – of spoken word in print has been one of the motivating forces behind this project. From absence comes the opportunity to shine a light on that which has been left behind and overlooked, to disrupt the dominant narrative of what 'page poetry' is, challenge the notion that 'accessibility' is a dirty word which some traditionalists equate to a rejection of craft, and to better represent and document the work of those poets who have been marginalised or subjected to 'voice poverty' in print.

Solid Air includes multi-disciplinary artists in every sense of the word: from full-time practising spoken word artists, national slam champions, veteran performance and sound poets, page poets who also work at times in a performative context, playwrights, musicians and songwriters, comedians, authors, journalists, children's writers, cabaret artists, actors, hip hop artists, essayists, filmmakers, spoken word MCs and poetry event convenors, theatre practitioners, zine makers, teachers, lecturers, festival directors, cultural producers, activists and a female rugby league prop. Some of these writers don't necessarily self-identify as a 'spoken word artist', yet we believe their work in some way falls under this large umbrella – all were willing to have their work take shelter within, from whatever it is that you can name as rain.

Ahakoa he iti he pounamu / Although it is small it is precious

We approached this project with a broad remit: to play and curate without the constraint of absolutes. Our intent was to ensure that this was not an anthology by poets for poets. *Solid Air* builds on us having curated festivals in the past with an intent to push poetry outwards into possibility. We have gone open-eared to open mics, to poetry slams, to multi-platform performances, to YouTube, Twitter and audio files on repeat. All the while chasing lucid dreams of a live line that once broke us. Or haunted us after the lights went down.

The enormity of this task was daunting: there is no real precedent in this region; the seminal *Off the Record* released way back in 1983 being the only time anyone has attempted to comprehensively anthologise performance poetry in Australia. As co-editors, it feels as though the threads we've woven together could have created a net large enough to cast across the *moana* between Australia and Aotearoa New Zealand. As you hold *Solid Air* in your hand, this book may seem as small as a shell by the shoreline considering what it is attempting to do: document the vastness of spoken word across the two countries for the past ten years. Like a shell, we can only ask that you place it close to your ear and listen.

'When we make "Spoken Word" a noun, it encompasses text and music. Performance Poetry, Live Poetry, Living Poetry, Performed Poetry, Hip Hop, Spoken Word; it is here you find that hollow muscular organ keeping poetry alive.' — Andrew Galan

We believe there is nothing concrete about what can be housed under spoken word's roof, despite the efforts of some town planners to review the form's foundation blueprint and have it rezoned or subdivided. These efforts have only shown us what spoken word is not: it is not exclusive, bound by the page or stage, or by poetry itself. It is not based in the academy, the academic, HECS approved, or colonised by a Western canon. It is not owned by or at the behest of a literary landlord, nor is it expensive to renovate or always able to pay rent on time. It is not an exact science and cannot be held under a light. It doesn't require a book or an anthology to justify its rightful place amongst the seagulls seeking the stray hot chip we call art.

The pieces within this collection have their own agency and spirit, we have merely invited them into this space to create a place where they can join as a chorus and amplify each other. There is not one poetry or poetry audience; there are many, and all of them are welcome to enter here. *Solid Air* is not only a gateway to the multiplicities of poetry available in our region – it is a house in which poetry resides, a speculative investment, constructed from open windows and unlocked doors.

The beautiful ocean

HANI ABDILE

This beautiful ocean was once a nightmare to me
Blue water and blue sky were blended and darkness was produced
Salty and foggy smoke was the air I inhaled
And if I could colour my fear it would be red
A danger zone, a chemical home and prohibited human zone

This beautiful ocean was once a nightmare to me
Life went without meaning
Shocked human
Eyes without sight
A dry mouth
The earth beneath us was enemies of waves
Crashing like the tectonic plate
Our hope has already crashed away

This beautiful ocean was once a nightmare to me
But I was the captain of my actions
I embraced my bravery not my destination
And as the days passed
Australia came close
A lavish land full of life
Dolphins marching
Like the armies on Anzac Day

This beautiful ocean
Was once my escaping cage
It was where I sought refuge
She really cares at some point
Because she protected me
From the wild creatures she gives shelter

And this world is a playground
Where humans are toys
And life is full of exams
This beautiful ocean
Taught me how to appreciate

And right at this moment
When I come closer to her
Silence overtakes my brain
She says, Do you remember me?
I am only good for visits not long journeys
The sand whispers welcome home
As I wrote this poem I was not far away from her
Her cool breeze gently inspired me to write
She is kind for a short time but not for long journey

Landmarks

JESSICA ALICE

All day I try to talk out the question
of my unknown self, as if its
invocation will dissolve the membrane
between my waking life – limestone
and mahogany city – and the underworld,
where I lay one languid leg.

Everything that I tell you is a gift
at the Baron's altar – black coffee,
rum, cigar – and I offer you my naked
wrist so I may grip your flesh
to carry between watery dimensions.

Cities go in every other direction –
flight paths from underneath
the fuselage – and you return
to a waking context, landscape demarcations.

I take my body out to practise
a little grace, by fire
and icons, and my desire ricochets
with the speed and frequency
of a hummingbird. For weeks
my heart has been going
at this rate and you remind me
of punctuation – breath
rising a slow burn

This pleasure state is not made
only for me and my solipsism so
I look for reasons to travel outside
myself and the known sides of satellites.
I hope to leave only kind impressions
on this map but my instinct is expressed
in visible marks and I haven't left
any on you yet.

(Because I am a daughter) of diaspora

EUNICE ANDRADA

and by default –
an open sea,
what language will not meet me
with rust?

They convince my mother
her voice is a selfish tide,
claiming words that are not meant
for her;

this roiling carcass of ocean
making ragdolls of our foreign limbs.

In the end our brown skin
married to seabed.

When I return to the storm
of my islands
with a belly full of first world,
I wrangle the language I grew up with
yet still have to rehearse.
I play with the familiar rattle of consonants
on my tongue and do not think myself
a serpent.

By the street corner, a man in rags
speaks to me in practised English.
Where are you going?

I don't respond,
the words a recognition
of the mongrel flag
I call my face.
I want to say to him, *We are the same.*
Pareho lang po tayo.

My bleached accent,
the dollars in my wallet
sing another anthem.

How long have you been here?

How long are you staying?

I am above water, holding
onto a country that drowns
with or without me.

Fern your own gully
EVELYN ARALUEN

Deep in the heart of the forest   there's a magical world
     where wonderous creatures
         plaaay the daaay awaaay

And an unusual girl
dreams of faraway places   dreams of cassette radio   of blond boys
of defensible monarchies
     is comfortable with poetic forms of entanglement
and likes the smell of eucalypt

When she flew where   no one had flown before
     there were huge! discoveries!
she used her powers   (she has powers)
she rescued the blond boy   she rescued the forest
she is crowned in f l o w e r i n g b l o s s o m
         and all other holy things

     Deep in the trees:
The orni-thorhyn-chus-ana-tinus sings affectation
the eyelashed mama roo opens her pouch
the koala collects   his gumnut coins   his sugarbush comb
a fresh change of unmentionables and they all swag jollily off to the coronation

Just hop in that pouch, unusual girl
hop in the swag   this whole home waits
in handpainted frames of silk native frocks
     wear them to your reading
     wear wattles from your ears
it's all metaphor for   the beautiful thin white woman
whose body slides linenly through bush
     the notion that when my straggly brown strips from the tree
     that it will be the smooth glow of ghost gum beckoning
it can't be lyric if you're   flora, right?
it can't be sovereign if you're   fauna, right?

Unusual girls fuck up their dendrology
cos they didn't come to bushcare
fern up the gully girls
go live those pastel bush dreams
while me and my ancestors sit   pissed swinging on the veranda couch

     RIGHT   WHERE   YOU   WROTE   US!

Godbox
KEN ARKIND

'I have lived to thank God, that all my prayers have not been answered.' — Jean Ingelow

I found these.

Tucked between the pages of phone books and bibles, beneath hospital pillows, the bottoms of whiskey bottles, inside garage sale-baby shoes. In all the places we feel closest to you.

Just some suggestions.

Can I maybe lose about 20 pounds?

Invent a popsicle that licks you back.

I know she lives in your neighbourhood, so maybe next time you see her, could you tell my mum to call me?

Some things to make it easier on everyone.
Because we need more proof that you exist than burning trees.
Anyone can start fires, it's putting them out that's the problem, but you would know all about that, wouldn't you?

Can you turn my tits into a sports page?
Then maybe my husband will look at me again.

Babies that shake parents back.

Please let Grandma die already.
She misses Grandpa so much
and I'm so tired of hearing about it.

It's not that we mean to be selfish.
It's just that we are.
It's been a long time since that last miracle,
and your boy doesn't count.

Please make Kanye West stop doing dumb shit.

A sky that's always turned to the sunset channel?

Could you make this wheelchair feel like my father's shoulders?

Invent a make-up that prevents bruises instead of just covering them up.

You got donuts, and you got the fucking donut holes ...
well then how about just giving me the
WHOLE GODDAMN DONUT AT THE SAME TIME!!

we just took advantage of him.

Just imagine if you had sent a daughter.

Invent a wedding ring that he can't take off.

Give me back my brother's last thought. That one belongs to me.

Tangle my hair one last time before the chemo takes it away.

Please be negative, please be negative, please be negative ...

Please let the Red Sox win. He always uses the belt when they lose ...

What do you do with all of your fan mail?
Do you actually read it, or do you just use the paper
to pick the corpses from between your teeth?

Hail Mary's that solve problems as well as bullets do.

Never let me grow up to be as fat and ugly as my mother is now.

Just for once, could I wake up to the sound
of church bells outside of my window,
instead of gunshots?

You understand English! Why can't they?

FUCK YOU.

Please let her be too drunk to remember my face in the morning.

If we were created in your own image
then how can you stand the sight of yourself?
How many mirrors have you broken?
As we fire our guns at the sky, mistaking demands
for prayers, not expecting you to shoot us back.

Please, shoot us back.

Don't let my daughter's new boyfriend be black.

FUCK YOU!

FUCK YOU!

Couldn't you have made my son a retard instead of queer?

FUCK YOU!

FUCK YOU.

FUCK YOU.

11

Because I have called, and ye refused; I have stretched out my hand, and no man regarded; So I too will laugh at your calamity; I will mock when your fear cometh; When your fear cometh as desolation, and your destruction cometh as a whirlwind; Then they shall call upon me, but I will not answer; they shall call upon me, but I will not answer; I will not answer.

—*Proverbs 1:24–28*

Are you listening?

Can you hear me?

Are you there?

Three reasons for sleeping with a white man
TUSIATA AVIA

tasi

I thought it would be like the border crossing.
I slept with him and dreamt I was sleeping
with him and waking in a room full of children
wearing European shoes.

lua

I thought he might rub off on me.
I slept with him and dreamt he was calling me
his Polynesian Princess.

On the wall the velvet maiden
turns a green shoulder
repositions her hibiscus
and smiles.

tolu

I thought Eh, what the hell
and opened my legs
(not my eyes).

I dreamt I was leaving his house
and all my family were standing outside
my cousin married to her American pilot
my mother
my brother looking like a Maori.
I kissed them all, they kissed me back
even my brother
I asked them
what they were doing.

They asked me
Suga, what are
you
doing?

A brief guide to hijab fashion
MARYAM AZAM

For an elegant look that won't fall apart
during those long hours at school, uni or work,
try a laff scarf, wrapped once around the head:

pin one end by the ear and bring the other
across to conceal the shape of your bust
and discreetly fasten onto the shoulder.
(Note: add a flower brooch or statement
 headband to jazz up the look.)

When fine dining
or a friend's party calls for some bling,
or the hippie in you wants to show off
some tribal earrings, tie the scarf at the back
of your head, wrap one end across

and back over your bun and pin in place.
Bring the other end across your chest and secure.
(Note: a large bun will keep the scarf in place –
use a 'volumising scrunchie' to boost bun size.)

In the middle of a Sydney summer
when the seatbelt stings to touch
keep cool in the khaleeji aka Dubai style:
let the scarf billow as you wrap it loosely around the face;
hold in place with a headband. The resulting

soft drapes frame the face and fall across
the chest like a curtain of cloud.
Feel like a desert princess. (Note: engineer
even drapes with a few discreet pins.)

If you'd like to wear a silk square scarf
without it slipping off your head
the minute you move away from the mirror,
may we recommend the Turkish style:
folded in half, pinned under the chin,

wrapped around the neck for definition
and tucked in or fanned out across the chest.
Turkish women like to pin any folds down
for a sleek, defined profile.
(Note: suits women with round faces best.)

For that poolside Bali resort-chic
look no further than the turban style:
pull on a ninja cap to cover a bare neck
and tuck in hair, then twist-tie two ends

of a rectangular scarf behind your neck
(like a bandana), before wrapping the pieces
over and around the head. (Note: to avoid
overheating use a light, breathable cotton scarf.)

For soccer training, quick supermarket trips,
or when unexpected guests drop by,
go for our no fuss one-piece ready-made scarves.
Available in cool cotton or stretch jersey,
plain, patterned, ruffled, sequined

these scarves simply slip over your head
and you're done. No pinning required.
(Note: perfect for bad scarf days.)

If I had to sing
HINEMOANA BAKER

I have no idea what to call this rebirth
and yet I'm here to name it
to feed the new flame

with wood from the old.
Language is a flute, a lily
a chair overbalancing;

a church we teeter
on the threshold of.
There are places where

they harvest water from the air —
drink fog from a glass then overnight
hang the rag back on the bayonet.

Does a thing which is reborn
need to have died?
All those cities still live

in my mirrors, they rise
and fall again with the sun's
rounds, the way the planet

carves its own seismic
trench in the solar system.
The spring charges

and recharges its river system
while on the columns of our lives
press unimaginable stresses.

Hold me up now, as I do you.
Sing, and steady me under
your strong, sure feet.

Depreston
COURTNEY BARNETT

You said we should look out further, I guess it wouldn't hurt us
We don't have to be around all these coffee shops
Now we've got that percolator, never made a latte greater
I'm saving twenty-three dollars a week

We drive to a house in Preston, we see police arrestin'
A man with his hand in a bag
How's that for first impressions? This place seems depressing
It's a Californian bungalow in a cul-de-sac

It's got a lovely garden, a garage for two cars to park in
Or a lot of room for storage if you've just got one
And it's going pretty cheap you say, well it's a deceased estate
Aren't the pressed metal ceilings great?

Then I see the handrail in the shower, a collection of those canisters for
    coffee, tea and flour
And a photo of a young man in a van in Vietnam
And I can't think of floorboards anymore, whether the front room faces
    south or north
And I wonder what she bought it for

If you've got a spare half a million
You could knock it down and start rebuildin'

If you've got a spare half a million
You could knock it down and start rebuildin'

If you've got a spare half a million
You could knock it down and start rebuildin'

If you've got a spare half a million
You could knock it down and start rebuildin'

If you've got a spare half a million
You could knock it down and start rebuildin'

If you've got a spare half a million
You could knock it down and start rebuildin'

In my day (Nan)
THE BEDROOM PHILOSOPHER

In my day we used to walk to school
Five miles in the snow
Cocaine was everywhere

In my day we ate toast from a can
From Japan

In my day when it was cold
Father'd hop into bed with you
and set fire to his beard

In my day children were seen but not heard
They'd died!
They were all ghosts!
But you still had to work!

In my day
Things were better than they are now
(Where am I)

We made food out of flour and water
It really put a damper on things

We played a board game called Hard Times
Where every square said
Go To War

In my day we couldn't afford punctuation
motherimjustgoingdowntotheriver verywellthen
Was a typical conversation

In my day we kept sea horses
and land whales
I think they're called 'cows' now

In my day I rode a bicycle
Hooked up to a generator
Powering my life support!

In my day we slept standing up
and ate upside down

You got tied to a bull and sent away
Whoever untied you
Well that's who you married

In my day we used to listen to OURSELVES on the radio
It wasn't even on
We weren't well

In my day there was a saying
Where there's smoke there's salmon

In my day for Christmas we got a memory stick
It was just a stick and if you forgot something
Father'd hit you with it!

In my day
I knew where I lived
(What's my name)

Children are the orgasm of the world
HERA LINDSAY BIRD

This morning on the bus there was a woman carrying a bag with inspirational sayings and positive affirmations, which I was reading because I'm a fan of inspirational sayings and positive affirmations. I also like clothing that gives you advice. What's kinder than the glittered baseball cap of a stranger telling you what to strive for? It's like living in a world of endless therapists. The inspirational bag of the woman on the bus said a bunch of stuff like 'live in the moment' and 'remember to breathe', but it also said 'children are the orgasm of the world'. Are children the orgasm of the world like orgasms are the orgasms of sex? Are children the orgasm of anything? Children are the orgasm of the world like hovercraft are the orgasm of the future or silence is the orgasm of the telephone, or shit is the orgasm of the lasagne. You could even say sheep are the orgasm of lonely pastures, which are the orgasm of modern farming practices, which are the orgasm of the industrial revolution. And then I thought why not? I like comparing stuff to other stuff too. Like sometimes when we're having sex and you look like a helicopter in a low-budget movie, disappearing behind a cloud to explode. Or an athlete winning a prestigious international sporting tournament at the exact same moment they discover their wife has just been kidnapped. For the most part, orgasms are the orgasms of the world. Like slam-dunking a glass basketball. Or executing a perfect dive into a swimming pool full of oh my god. Or travelling into the past to forgive yourself and creating a time paradox so beautiful it forces all of human history to reboot, stranding you naked on some distant and rocky outcrop, looking up at the sunset from a world so new looking up hasn't even been invented yet.

My housemate's girlfriend

AMY BODOSSIAN

They fuck into the hot, still night
her gasps ripe
full and overt
like her pendulous breasts
that were falling out of her cobalt blue dress
when she was standing in my kitchen
only about half an hour before
consoling my neurosis about our resident rat
that had just run across my bedroom floor
she assures me
I won't get a rash
she's so relaxed
as she shuts the door
on her and my housemate's love den

I perch on the edge of my bed
ruminating about possible infections
the rat runs through my head
I just can't let go.

Then, sitting at my computer,
I think of you
candles burn
each flame an attempt at solitude
my new calm life
candles and meditation CDs
the hot summer night
aches with suburban stillness
outside my bedroom window

And then I hear her
'Oh, oh, OH!'
moaning, as I so often do,
I knew they'd be having sex tonight
they're always having sex

At first I think maybe it's a car in the distance,
a howling dog, a siren perhaps?
It's kind of abstract
and indistinguishable
and of course it is a siren
but it's not that kind of vehicle, it's her –
her raw, intimate pleasure
wounding my bruised heart, each gasp
stabbing that place that wants to be loved,
each sigh searing that tender spot
that just wants to be hugged,
wants to be
filled.

I came quietly into my hand by candlelight
about ten minutes earlier,
humped a pillow and tried not to think of you
but no one else has entered that space yet
your face still fresh,
faded,
but I can still access it if I absolutely have to –
trying to remember
trying to forget
remember
forget
but remember,
not too much
just enough to make me come
get the job done
and then I lie
satisfied
spent
and pathetic

a tiny muted pebble in the huge night.

Forgive me my love
BEHROUZ BOOCHANI

Translated by Moones Mansoubi, Manus Island, Papua New Guinea, 2018

Forgive me my bird as I am not able to embrace you.
But here,
in this corner,
I know some migrating birds that I smile to at dawn.
I embrace them with open arms,
as open as the immensity of the sky.

My beautiful love!
Forgive me as I am not able to drink the aroma of your breath,
but here, in the ruins of this prison,
wildflowers grow each morning in my heart
and in the dead of night they drift into sleep with me, where I rest.

Forgive me my angel!
As I am not able to caress your gentle skin with my fingertips.
But I have a lifelong friendship with the zephyr
and those gentle winds from the sea strum my bare skin here in this tropical purgatory.
Forgive me, as I am not able to climb the verdant mountains of your body,
but here, in the depths of darkness, always at midnight, I enjoy deep and utter seclusion
among the tall and dignified coconut trees.

25

My beautiful! I sing to you the profundities of the most ancient and enigmatic songs,
far away from the world, a man loves you from within the deepest oceans and the darkest forests.
Inside a cage,
the man loves you,
inside a cage located between the vastest ocean and the densest jungle …

Forgive me my love as I am solely able to love you from a remote island,
inside a cage,
from the corner of this small room.
Forgive me please as the only part of the world that belongs to me are these fragments.

26

To the flight attendant on QF11 to LA

C.J. BOWERBIRD

To the flight attendant on QF11 to LA:
James,
It might be the red wine you poured so
conscientiously, casually splashing two drops so you could
confide how the turbulent tremors appear at always the
wrong time, causing us to spill when we mean to
contain, but the fourteen hours I spent with your eyes have
changed me. James,

your eyes blue like Lake Louise,
condemned to ever imitate the pristine Rocky Mountain
peaks but never free enough to
disturb them, those tall sharp points
dangerously tempting, right there,
out of reach. James,

your eyes blue like glacier cracks,
opening like wardrobe doors to
timeless tundras of beauty and numbing
amnesia, pitching forgotten wars of
lions and timid boys. James,

your eyes blue, wide,
contradictory like autumn skies, a weak
apology or a vow to return with
heat, posing the question that stands
pigeon-toed between innocence and deceit.

And I should know. I too have
blue eyes that sometimes knock on
unlocked doors, offer answers that sound like
requests, know far more than they
share with me. James,

it might be the red wine, but
fuck it, it's not the red wine,
it is the fourteen hours I spent with your
eyes that woke an idle part of me.

Ever since the moment I arrived in this world,
cold, I have been handed
bricks. I have placed them
conscientiously, building walls around my yard, glorious
hygienic mountain towers of safety and
distraction. But you reminded me of the
turbulent tremors that appear at always the
right time, that one brick left crooked and a
crack.

A crack that, if I lean forward and
peer, allows me to see into other meadows,
marvel at the reflection of my face in
someone else's lake. James,

your eyes reminded me that we are born human first,
naked over open fields, but
we are taught to lay tectonic
shields. James,

your eyes reminded me that we arrive with
wide, open sight, but we
fall between walls, we
labour to construct our Shangri-La. James,

thank you for reminding me that if we
crack open that little gap, we can
see very, very far.

fly in fly out fly in fly out
ALLAN BOYD (AKA THE ANTIPOET)

fly in fly out fly in fly out
and she's on another swing
a roundabout of airports
another pilbara narrative
racking up the qantas points
at the exit seat, inside a novel
pindan fingers
pindan boots
fly in fly out fly in fly out
siren, rumble of blast
iron hills to rubble
at the next CAT ONE shutdown
we evacuate ourselves
in a debt cycle
for a new house i'll never live in
a boat i'll never float
and fly in fly out fly in fly out
six years of missed birthday cake
skype in a donga on mothers day
can't talk with a mouthful of flies
on the tarmac haze, jet fuel stench
at hi-viz horizons, the bus at 5AM
another DandA test before dawn
one beer per man, open can
in the wet mess, scrolling screens
never drunk enough
to fly in fly out fly in fly out
in my box the
flint-eyed mirror
says get more sleep, smile
inside these thinnest walls
sounds of next door snore
another breath
to the beat of the air-con
the tv red glow, fridge hum

waiting for the alarm's pierce
fly in fly out fly in fly out
now lost in suburban streets
shopping centre carparks
peeling products from shelves
staring at labels, empty trolley
missing the truck hum
until she's on another swing
fly in fly out fly in fly out

Employment separation certificate
JAKOB BOYD (AKA LAUNDRY MAN)

I'd be so sick from staying up drinking
dreading work when I'd rock up in the morning
sick with beer sick with hunger and fear
I'd force myself to puke in the staff toilets
before getting into the beef fat stench
of last night's uniform

it took two hours to get there
two hours to get home

and those stolen vegie patties would go soggy in my bag

I'd stand around all day isolated
drive thru window dead midday air
making drink trays
digging deeper into the nothingness of heartbreak
until cigarette cravings
turned to panic attacks

Ford Falcon arsehole
begging for a bacon deluxe
with my chest stabbing in flux

and those stolen vegie patties would go soggy in my bag

on my days off
surfing counter culture galaxies
prophetic myths and poems on fire
in pan-dimensional inner-city lounge rooms
I was falling in love
with so many futures
philosophical pubs and alleyway brainwaves

smoking joints under docks down in Freo
waking up to plunge back
into the industrial salt shit beef systems of Clarkson
handing baby chicken corpses over the counter
in a safe liberal seat

and those stolen vegie patties would go soggy in my bag

no market to pray to
no gods on sale

eyeballs of impatient pricks
watching my every
minute movement

3 o'clock I'd be screaming
at a hundred after-school teens
no more of your
favourite colour of frozen coke

I'd chainsmoke through my breaks
till I was light-headed

and those stolen vegie patties would go soggy in my bag

for rocking up late
however many times
from all night binge treaties
in community gardens

I got the sack

now I get such hard blues
down here in the Centrelink queues

Dear Mrs Miller
JESSE JOHN BRAND

Dear Mrs Miller
Do you remember when your son Sam and I were seven
and you told us
we were made of fire?
That these atoms were fashioned where the hearts of stars dwell
nebulas cascading through our veins and epithelial cells

Dear Mrs Miller
Do you remember when you said we learn history
so we never summon a Delphic phoenix from Dresden's lungs
toppled cities burning for the Guernica drums
Berlin yearning for oblivion until obsidian comes
ruptured in rapture
hearts, minds and balls captured
around the tongue of Damocles
iridium hung
we never repeat it

Dear Mrs Miller
When Sam and I were fifteen we smoked joints in backyards
when we were sixteen we were slangin' shards
this kidnapped generation left home
found a hallway in our veins
that led to a doorway in our brains
that opened to oblivion
and Stockholm syndrome

~~In my mind it keeps repeating~~
~~In my mind it keeps repeating~~
~~Keeps repeating~~
the beating of a door
where Benzedrine dreams ignite
Seraphim silence cyclones in the psilocybin night
Parepin swallowed
remoulded and fucked

the sky's what we were aiming for when we were shooting up
Sam pushed that doorway into the eternal black
and one day he walked
down that hallway
and he never came back

you said we were made of fire

~~Dear Mrs Miller, I owned the stardust that killed your son.~~

Dear Mrs Miller, I ~~owned the stardust that~~ killed your son.

But if the atoms in the stars are in the ones we've loved and lost
then isn't it possible
that someday
those same atoms
could be split to summon
nuclear holocaust?
Was Hiroshima another broken heart?
For him
I'd fashion Armageddon into a human being again

Please never forgive me
my halo is spun with barbed wire
but if you seek me
I'll be scaling
the infinity spires

Dear Mrs Miller
Tonight the stars look alive
like Dresden on fire

Moko
BEN BROWN

Take a look at my face
Got the right shape
for the moko
Got the haughty jut
to the jaw
Got an appropriate nose
for the koru bro

I got borstal stars
and a crooked cross
But I never been inside eh
They just bullshit schoolboy tats
Idiot stickers cost me nothing
but an inky needle and
some discomfort

Yeah but I wear my moko
on the inside bro
Old-school chiselling
in pigment and blood
cut with an albatross bone

This line is my father's line
This line is my mother's
Here is a mountain
A river
A suburb
Here is the chanting karakia
of a young man bleeding
beneath the blade
Tat-tat-tat-tat
Tat-tat-tat-tat

Here is a road in the footsteps of a warrior
Here is a path in the broken feet of a slave

My VICES
EDDY BURGER

I was walking down the street, minding my own (**COFFEE!**) business, when I see this person I know, and he (**COFFEE!**) comes up to me and tells me I'm not looking well, says I'm looking (**CIGARETTES!**) tense, says I've got dark smudges under my eyes. I tell him I'm all right, and I manage to get away, only to be confronted by (**CIGARETTES!**) someone else I know. She says I look weary, says I should take better (**CIGARETTES!**) care of myself and should try to lead a (**SUGAR!**) healthier lifestyle. I'm (**COFFEE!**) doing all right, I say. I eat (**SUGAR!**) well. But I'm in a hurry, I say, I have to make a (**COFFEE!**) business appointment. I dash around the nearest corner, pass the (**CIGARETTES!**) local health-food store, and slip into a (**SUGAR!**) café. I take a seat. I call for a (**COFFEE!**) waiter. But just as the waiter comes over, three people I know – people who (**FATTY FOOD!!**) work in the health-food store – come over (**SUGAR!**) and ask if they can (**CIGARETTES!**) join me. Certainly, I say. The (**FATTY FOOD!!**) waiter looks at me. My acquaintances look at me. I order (**CIGARETTES!**) a felafel roll and a glass of (**COFFEE!**) celery juice. They say (**FATTY FOOD!!**) that I should (**OIL!**) take better care of my (**SUGAR!**) body, I (**CIGARETTES!**)(**OIL!**) should exercise (**FATTY FOOD!!**) more, do I suffer from (**CIGARETTES!**) stress? am I (**COFFEE!**)(**SUGAR!**)(**FATTY FOOD!!**) getting enough (**OIL!**) sleep? (**COFFEE!**)(**CIGARETTES!**)(**SUGAR!**) (**FATTY FOOD!!**)(**OIL!**) and I really should take better care of myself.

What is your ceiling?

PASCALLE BURTON

From the United States War Department's Restricted Japanese Phrase Book, *1944*

please come in (please come in)
please sit down (please sit down)
COME IN!
SIT DOWN!
   HERE!
   THERE!

make yourself comfortable (make yourself comfortable)
will you have a cigarette? (do you have a light?)
are you —? (are you —?)
   hungry?
   thirsty?
please come with me
COME WITH ME!

I want to ask you questions
please answer yes or no
ANSWER YES OR NO!
please show me
SHOW ME!
please write it
WRITE IT!
please write the number
WRITE THE NUMBER!
please tell the truth
TELL THE TRUTH!
you will not be hurt (you will not be hurt)
you will be rewarded

is the water deep?
are the mountains high?
is the current swift?

is there a bridge?
where can I find a mechanic?
what is your ceiling?

WAIT HERE!
STAND UP!
COME FORWARD!
RIGHT AWAY!
MOVE BACK!
TURN AROUND!
GO AHEAD!
FOLLOW ME!
FOLLOW HIM!
GO SLOW!
HURRY!
DON'T SHOOT!
HALT!
WHO IS THERE?
ADVANCE!

IDENTIFY YOURSELF! (identify yourself)
DON'T MOVE!
SURRENDER!
THROW DOWN YOUR ARMS!
RAISE YOUR HANDS!
LINE UP!
    LINE UP HERE!
    LINE UP THERE!
DON'T TRY ANY TRICKS!
OBEY OR I'LL FIRE!

is the water deep?
are the mountains high?
is the current swift?
is there a bridge?
where can I find a mechanic?
what is your ceiling?

Maury Wiseman
RHYAN CLAPHAM (AKA DOBBY)

No wonder the word 'Aboriginal' invisible
I'm learning all my history from pictures in a picture book
Covered it in principle was taught not to be critical
Tested on the people is it written is it physical?

And if I dismiss it I'll be sent up to the principal
The shit's already published but my story the residual
Dissing evidence as a measurement call it mythical
Evident intent of the detriment of the Bidjigal

Back and forth on the narrative like a pendulum
God forbid they mention they mention the massacres in curriculum
Who they mentioning? 'It's embarrassing all your blemishes
and after all you ain't a damn pack of Native Americans'

'And shit we practise an Aboriginal welcoming
come on I mean we've had it you savages think you're everything'
'Don't you know my daddy grand-daddy used to be legendary
protector of the blacks so I'm practically Aborigine'

That's the shit that is naturally condescending people
Arrogant to think we just asking for every penny
      (OR: That's the shit that is naturally condescending it's the
      casual dismissal of Aboriginal history)

In fact we think the betterment of blackness is irrelevant but
'After all you ain't a pack of African Americans'

I'm black. No matter what a white person telling me
We walking altogether all as one, like a centipede
Wanna talk about me listen up and learn my history
But fuck a school textbook, that shit be elementary

Wanna talk about me listen up and learn my history
But fuck a school textbook, that shit be elementary
(Maury Wiseman)

Wanna talk about me listen up and learn my history
But fuck a school textbook, that shit be elementary

Your policy is money my policy in the wallaby
Land is like a loan but you wanting to make monopoly
Eventually we'll fuckin' rape the world of its forestry
Ain't a tree around, so I'm knocking on mahogany

Closing a community to them it's like a robbery
Mining in the Kimberley to land it's like sodomy
Cut the black story from the news, that's lobotomy
And talk about the blacks to their backs, that's politics

My Aboriginality is stuck in anthropology
But we still alive and kicking like a soccer team
Always told me there was something fuckin' wrong with me
Eight-year-old girl suicide, that's a problem

Our culture is everlong and our history not forgotten
But damnit we need support in the journey into equality
So learn from us, listen up with empathy
But fuck a school textbook that shit be elementary

Wanna talk about me listen up and learn my history
But fuck a school textbook, that shit be elementary
(Maury Wiseman)
Wanna talk about me listen up and learn my history
But fuck a school textbook, that shit be elementary

Bitch I'm Maury Wiseman on the track I mean,
Me and Barry Spurr, we the magic team,
So tell it like it is, tell it like it is,
Nobody up in here that can manage me

Bitch I'm Maury Wiseman on the track I mean,
Me and Barry Spurr, we the magic team,
Get the fuck outta my class, boy!
Nobody here above me that can manage me

Sigrid Sassoon: The Prime Minister
JOHN CLARKE

*Profoundly affected by her experience of war, Sigrid exposed its horrors and
expressed undisguised contempt for those politicians who stayed home, doing
nothing to stop it.*

'Good morning, good morning,' the PM lied,
as he paused on the doorstep and turned to the press.
He was saddened, he said, that some children had died,
in his rocket attacks, which were such a success.
'It's hard to avoid,' he told Lawsie and Jones,
as they both went out 'live' on their satellite phones,
'... if people build schools in our targeting zones.'

gil scott-heron is on parole
MAXINE BENEBA CLARKE

gil scott-heron / is on parole
    revolution
gil scott-heron / is on parole

gil scott-heron / is on parole
    believe it
gil scott-heron / is on parole

we last saw gil tryin to flee the country
the revolution was packed flat
between powdered bank note wads
claustrophobic / packed in his navy canvas tote

what in the hell was gil scott thinkin
with that feisty revolution hollerin
like beelzebub broke loose
oh gil / what were you thinkin
of course the cops were gonna notice you

the revolution was screamin
   let me outta here gil scott
   i swear / progress is being made
   ain't it progress: a black man
   headin for that white house over yonder
   lemme loose godammit gil scott
   i wanna witness it
the revolution said

   believe it
gil scott-heron is on parole

believe it
gil scott-heron
    oh yeah: parole

    shut the fuck up
gil told the revolution
    cause brother that false bravado
    is tired and old

    revolution
gil scott-heron is on parole

kanye / elephunk
and missy feat timbaland
are somehow all involved
and a new cradle full of brown kids
will finally be allowed a soul
cause brothers and sisters
gil scott-heron is on parole
he's sorted out his shit
and all last night was in his studio

glory be

all our sons and daughters
can now swing low / hold on tight
little pickneys / cause here comes brother gil
to carry y'all home

lift the needle from the turnin table

    revolution

hush the crowds
and mic the phone

    revolution

bring the djembe snorin in the store room
and please somebody
dust off the throne

ain't nobody heard the news

    revolution

gil scott-heron is comin home

I am the road
CLAIRE G. COLEMAN

My grandfather was the bush, the coast, salmon gums, hakeas, blue-grey
    banskias
Wind-whipped water, tea-black estuaries, sun on grey stone
My grandfather was born on Country, was buried on Country
His bones are Country
I am the road

I was born off Country, in that city
I hear, less than two-weeks old I travelled Country
A bassinet on the back seat of the Kingswood
I remember travels more than I remember a home
I am the road

My father is the beach, the peppermint tree, the city back when, before it
    was a city
My father is the ancient tall-tree Country, between his father Country and
    that town
My father is World War II, his father was a soldier
My father wandered, worked on rail, drove trucks
I am the road

Campgrounds up and down that coast were the childhood home of my heart
Where my memories fled, where my happiness lived
Campgrounds in somebody else's stolen Country
I am the road

The road unrolls before me
My rusty old troopy wipes oily sweat from it's underside on the asphalt
Says, 'I am here, I am here'
The engine breathes in, breathes out, pants faster than I can
Sings a wailing thundering song
Wraps its steel self around me and keeps me safe, a too large overcoat
I am the road

I slept, for a time, on the streets of Melbourne
No Country, no home, as faceless as the pavement
I was dirt on the streets, as grey as the stone, as the concrete
I am the road

We showed explorers where the water was
They lay their road over our path, from water to water
Lay a highway over their road, tamed my Country with their highway
I am the road

My Boodja has been stolen, raped, they dug it up, took some of it away
They killed our boorn, killed our yonga, our waitch, damar, kwoka
Put in wheat and sheep, no country for sheep my Boodja
My Country, most of it is empty, the whitefellas have no use for it
Except to keep it from us
Because we want it back, need it back, because they can
I am the road

People ask where I am from, I cannot, simply answer
To mob, I am Noongar, South Coast. I am Banksias, wind on waves on stone
To travellers, whitefella nomads, I am from where I live – that caravan
    over there
To whitefellas from Melbourne who see how I drink my coffee
I must be from Melbourne, I am not Melbourne
I am the road

One day wish to, hope to, dream, buy some of my grandfather's Country
    back
Pay the thieves for stolen goods
Theft is a crime, receiving stolen goods is a crime
Until one day
I am the road.

Love is not love
JENNIFER COMPTON

1.
It was never love. Not love. It was
what the Italians call the thunderbolt.

We stared. We exchanged eyes. It
was easy. Not what we might have

wanted. Not what we had planned.
Many things were snatched away

like thistledown in the high and gusty
winds of our home town. Many things

arrived like the burden of a new language.
As if the kaleidoscope had been given a

vigorous shake and fallen into a new pattern.
And then broken. We shuddered, and woke.

2.
I saw fear in his eyes, but we stepped forward,
we took hands, just like lovers do, the ceremony

wound up with the pragmatic certainty of a dream.
The children stirred and knew it was nearly time.

The words we said shook us to the bone. Who knew
that words could be so precise, that we would mean

exactly what we said? Or that we would misunderstand
so much. Be lost forever, and yet, suddenly, be home.

The man and woman staring past each other in the street.
Angry and miserable, while sharing the exact same thought.

3.

We were given the years, then they were taken from us.
We arched an eyebrow each, the windward side of bitter.

Like two trees growing too close together to be separated
root and branch entangled – until one of us should die –

we could not grow closer to each other but grew away,
flourishing on the far side. If it was like music it was like

the music at the concert – do you remember? – where
we found ourselves without design, and the high, clear

pulse of your thought examining the invisible vibration
became all of the music for me. With you, I am alone.

Tramlines

ARIELLE COTTINGHAM

Let us pray.

I'm sitting on the 19 tram in Melbourne or Galveston Beach in Texas or any airport in the world and a stranger, usually a woman, asks WOW YOUR HAIR'S SOOOOOO CURLY – DO YOU EVER STRAIGHTEN IT? I think of my driver licence. I'm 18 with a puka shell necklace straight hair unrecognisable. I tell her no I tell her I like my curls, that my mother blessed me with them.

Let us give thanks.

She gets awkward, like she knows she crossed a straight line, asking if I ever tried to look whiter.

Let us pray.

I show any friend the driver licence. They say WOW THAT DOESN'T LOOK LIKE YOU AT ALL. I tell them my dad always liked it when I straightened my hair.

Peace be with you,
and also with you.

They get awkward like they don't wanna go through the daddyissues door I've just cracked open.

In the name of the Father,
let us pray.

I'm 18 and the holy blow dryer has pulled all the curls out of my hair for the week. My dad says YOU LOOK SO PRETTY WITH STRAIGHT HAIR. I tell him nothing because he hopes it'll make me feel better. YOU LOOK SO PRETTY WITH STRAIGHT HAIR YOU LOOK SO PRETTY WITH STRAIGHT HAIR YOU LOOK SO PRETTY WITH

STRAIGHT HAIR YOU LOOK SO PRETTY STRAIGHT.

In the name of the Father,
let us pray.
I'm 18 at a school track meet when pinched lips and freckles hit me like a lightning bolt from God and I cross the straight finish line fourth and she's too gorgeous for me to notice any of the boys.

In the name of the Father,
let us pray.
I'm 18 and Catholic wishing I was straight wishing I was straight wishing my hair was straight so my parents could love me more. YOU LOOK SO PRETTY WHEN YOU'RE STRAIGHT YOU LOOK SO PRETTY WHEN YOU'RE STRAIGHT PRETTY STRAIGHT PRETTY STRAIGHT. I'm pretty straight since I only ever bring men home. I'm pretty straight when my mum convinces me to straighten my hair one more time so my boyfriend can see it straight. Look how straight it gets look how straight I can be Mum just like you. *Peace be with you* with your straight hair *and also with you* and your straight marriage. I thought I wanted to be just like you Mum but I can't.

Let us pray.
Can't
Let us pray.
Can't
Let—

50

can't not have these consecrated curls, these holy river bends meandering in and out and in and out of straightness

In the name of the Father,
let us pray.
I'm sitting on the 19 tram in Melbourne.
It goes straight up Sydney Road.
No one here's asked about my hair today.

Peace be with you,
and also with you.
In the name of the Fath— no.
In the name of the Lapsed Daughter,
Amen.

I took my girl to see Eraserhead
DAMIAN COWELL

I met her in 'Dystopian hell
(… in post-war Cinema' – it was a university tute).
I thought if I could say 'Luis Buñuel'
enough times I might be half chance for a root.
She smoked Gitane in her funky bedsit
as she philosophised on urban dread.
We were young and beautiful and full of shit.
It was going so well – and then I took my girl to see *Eraserhead*.

I took my girl to see *Eraserhead*.

I went for the old 'theatrical yawn'
(you know the one, where you lean across and go for the pash?)
But on the screen there was this weird shit going on.
I was drawn like it was some kind of J.G. Ballard car crash.
People with papier mâché heads.
It was all apocalyptically sooty.
Roasted quail with jerking legs
and a deformed baby that looked like a … footy?

I lost my appetite for AFL.
Never ate KFC from that day on.
My libido was strangely quelled.
I thought it was going to be a rom-com!
I changed the subject when she wanted sex.
Now I imagined her rolling over in bed.
And whispering, 'That was Kafka-esque'.
It put me right off – cos I took my girl to see *Eraserhead*.

I took my girl to see *Eraserhead*.

What does it all mean? They scratch their beards.
Writing thousands of words, God, pinch me.
I can summarise it in three: 'People are weird.'
Tell us something we didn't know, Lynchy.

I broke up with her, it was really poor form.
She took it bad – I must have made no sense.
Fifteen years later my friend saw her
at a chartered accountants' conference.
She seemed quite normal and friendly too,
till he caught a glimpse of something odd. He said:
'The rubber on her pencil looked sort of like you.'
But surely you don't think that that had anything to do
with the fact that I took my girl to see *Eraserhead*?

I took my girl to see *Eraserhead*.

Spooks
EMILY CROCKER

I, a ghost of myself (groans and all), and you, cumbersome
with so much opacity. Itching in the aisles of hangers.
Each point of contact enacting a five-star violence
they don't know to call a violence; grinning and belted.
Glitching in the aisles,   mate   ah   *ma'am.*
I knew I was a ~~worry~~man when I began using my form
as a floatation device,   a skeleton key,   a dustpan –
corrections in neat brushwork *v, v, v, v, v   v, v, v, v, v*
I knew you were really *alive* each time your body
ingested the words   a lie,   a lie,   a lie,   like
snips of red felt by the traitor   ah,   *tailor*
placing pins in the lack of it all. Grief is a puncture in the lobe
that never quite closes – a moaning *o,   o,   o,   o,   o*
How desirous you are, at times,
to slip inside a different mass   like a lapel pin,
if it could only hold you close   ah   *closed*   ah   *clothed.*
All the while I am holding my~~breath~~self open
where I have nothing for you.   Which is to say, so much longing
it haunts us both. Undress yourself and slip inside my body,
elusive as it is, anytime you want to.

Corpse fete
NATHAN CURNOW

the corpse selling kisses at the kissing booth
a corn pipe jammed in its mouth
packed with mundungus and blue cheese
to overpower the stench of flesh
every stall holder is on ropes and pulleys
figurines in some dark fundraiser
two women at the urn in the coffee tent
dressed in mittens to hide the blisters
a fumbling of tongs at the sausage sizzle
balloons tied to the clown's remains
every lucky dip is a gift-wrapped finger
the face painter is receiving complaints
the stiff on the gate of the animal nursery
the dead float in the dunking chamber
red velvet cakes cannot be trusted
or the draw of the meat tray raffle
the fortune teller has dropped the ball
the sponge throw takes out an eye
nobody cares that they can see the ropes
no one finishes a whole toffee apple

My wedding dress
KORALY DIMITRIADIS

The day I moved out my stuff,
I took the wedding dress to Mum's house
the cardboard white coffin:

Crystallised Cynthia Briggs bridal gown
ivory silk, pulled up on one side with a flower,
purple tulle peeping through
the real me hidden under layers of antidepressants,
I had a big fat Greek wedding and my parents
were the happiest parents in the world.

Telling Mum I'm going to sell the dress on eBay,
Mum, taking the dress back, saying it's hers, she paid for it.
Watching her take it away to her room
to crawl into, sleep in for all eternity
'My life is over,' she said
'*Me evales ston tafo*'
You've put me in my grave

My wedding dress
My wedding dress

My country

TUG DUMBLY

Sorry Dorothea Mackellar

The love of truth and virtue
of humanitarian aims
of decency and justice
runs through other veins.
Compassion for the suffering
of folk from other skies
I know but cannot share it
my love is otherwise.

I love a stunted country
a land of weeping shame
of ragged locked-up strangers'
incarcerated pain.
I love her stubborn meanness
her fat-cat lawyer fees
her litigatious terror
of bindi-eye and bee.

Majestic old-growth forests
for whom the woodchip tolls
are chewed up to produce
a billion toilet rolls.
Put a planet on the barbie
those gas emissions thick
can melt the polar ice caps
like an esky brick.

Core of my heart, my country!
land of the handshake gold
where cash for comment shockjocks
fatten up their rolls
where flashy corporate swindlers

find greasy palms to oil
where pollie wants a kickback
and bankers scoff the spoils.

Core of my heart, my country!
her pitiless squalid lies
sick at heart surround us
thick as rancid flies.
But then an election gathers
and we can vote again
for some punchless little Judy
whose vision we sustain.

A flinty-hearted country
a compassion pinching land
built upon a bloodstain
we fail to understand.
It's black and white, cut and dyed
penned in our private sty:
'Bugger you, I'm right Jack'
the Lucky Country's lie.

What it's really like to grow up with lesbians in the 70s and 80s
QUINN EADES

You will go to your first peace march before you can walk.

You will say handy person, fire fighter, police officer, and automatically refer to all doctors as 'she' if their gender has not been defined.

Your favourite song when you are four will be 'Oh Bondage Up Yours!' by X-ray Spex.

You will not be allowed to shave your legs.

You will be able to use the word patriarchy in a sentence by the time you are five.

There will be NO eating of food from the Evil Empire. Don't say its name – we dare not speak its name.

When you turn eight, you will be given a cap with a picture of Mr Lazy on it with the words 'Mr Lazy' underneath the picture. You will simultaneously be given a silver pen (it was the eighties – there were silver pens everywhere) so that you can turn the Mr into a Ms.

You will not be allowed to wear pink. This will scar your sister for life.

When you turn nine, you will be given a book with line drawings in it on how to masturbate, and some of them will make your brain turn inside out.

When you start to bleed, you will be told about the dangers of tampons and toxic shock, and advised to always wear pads, but you will also be given a first edition of C.J. Dennis's

The Glugs of Gosh as a menstrual present.

When you start to bleed, you will not think you are dying because you knew about sex and reproduction and menstruation before you got to school.

You will assume that everyone goes to the toilet with the door open.

You will have at some point been vegetarian or vegan, and feel excessive guilt for not still being so.

You will ALWAYS have a compost heap.

You will probably know how to juggle, or toss a Diablo, or fire twirl.

When you are fourteen you will fall in love with your mother's girlfriend, and given there's nine years difference in age between you and her and fourteen years difference between her and your mother, you'll think you're in with a chance.

You will learn how to kiss girls at the Leichhardt Hotel women's pool comp when you are sixteen.

You will also become a VERY good pool player.

You will always have eleven types of tea in your cupboard, and four kinds of milk in your fridge.

Apart from your mother's girlfriend, you will also have crushes on Tracy Chapman, Suzanne Vega, the Indigo Girls, Cyndi Lauper, Kim Wilde and Joan Jett. And whenever you hear *you got a fast car* you'll get kinda mopey.

You will ALWAYS think that jeans and waistcoats are a good look.

You will be given trucks, blocks, books, or art supplies for every. single. birthday.

You will try to annoy your mother by wearing full leathers to her birthday party and getting your lip pierced, more than once.

You will try to annoy your mother by pretending you are heterosexual and bringing home the tallest, hairiest, dirtiest teenage boys you can find.

Your first tattoo will be deeply symbolic and will probably include a women's symbol or a labrys.

You will always resent the fact that you never got to come out.

You will be told you can be anything.

You will be loved. It will be a weird, kooky love that comes in bits and pieces from all corners and sometimes there will be too much and sometimes there will not be enough, but you will be loved.

And that's what it's like.

61

Yúya karrabúra (Fire is burning)
ALICE EATHER

I'm standing by this fire
the embers smoking,
the ashes glowing
the coals weighing us down
the youth are buried in the rubble
my eyes are burning
and through my nostrils the smoke is stirring

I breath it in.

(breath)

Yúya karrabúra

I wear a ship on my wrist that shows my blood comes from convicts
On the Second Fleet my fathers' forefathers came
whipped, beaten and bound in chains

The dark tone in my skin
the brown in my eyes
Sunset to sunrise my Wúrnal mother's side
My Kikka who grew up in a dugout canoe
in her womb is where my consciousness grew

Yúya karrabúra
I walk between these two worlds
a split life
split skin
split tongue
split kin

Everyday these worlds collide
and I'm living and breathing this story of black and white

Sitting in the middle of this collision
My mission is to bring two divided worlds to sit beside this fire and listen

Through this skin I know where I belong
it is both my centre
and my division

Yúya karrabúra

My ancestors dance in the stars
and their tongues are in the flames
and they tell me:

'You have to keep the fire alive
between the black and the white
there's a story waiting to be spoken
in every life there's a spirit waiting to be woken'

Now I'm looking at YOU with the stars in my eyes
and my tongue is burning flames

and I say

Yúya karrabúra

The sacred songs are still being sung
but the words are slowly fading
the distant cries I'm hearing are the mothers burying their babies
the Elders are standing strong
but the ground beneath them is breaking

Yúya karrabúra

Now I welcome you to sit beside my fire
I'm allowing you to digest my confusion
I will not point my finger and blame
'cause when we start blaming each other
we make no room for changing each other

and we've got to keep this fire burning
with ash on our feet
and coal in our hands
teach barrarodjibba – them young ones
how to live side by side

'Cause tomorrow when the sun rises
and our fires have gone quiet
they will be the ones who reignite it

Yúya karrabúra

And these flames – us
will be their guidance.

Circles & Squares
ALI COBBY ECKERMANN

I was born Yankunytjatjara My mother is Yankunytjatjara Her mother is
    Yankunytjatjara
My family is Yankunytjatjara

I have learnt many things from my Family Elders
I have grown to recognise that my life travels in Circles
My Aboriginal culture has taught me that
Universal life is Circular

When I was born I was not allowed to live with my Family
I grew up in the white man's world

We lived in a Square house
We picked fruit and vegetables from a neatly fenced Square plot
We kept animals in Square paddocks
We ate at Square tables
We sat on Square chairs
I slept in a Square bed

I looked at myself in a Square mirror and did not know who I was

One day I met my Mother
I just knew that this meeting was part of our Healing Circle
Then I began to travel
I visited places that I had been before
But this time I sat down with Family

We gathered closely Together by big Round campfires
We ate bush tucker feasting on Round ants and berries
We ate meat from animals that live in Round burrows
We slept in Circles on our beach around Our fires
We sat in the dirt on Our Land that belongs to a big Round planet
We watched the moon grow to a magnificent yellow Circle
That was our Time

I have learnt two different ways now
I am thankful for this
That is part of my Life Circle

My heart is Round like a drum ready to echo the Music of my Family

But the Square within me remains
The Square stops me in my entirety

Taranaki bitter
DAVID EGGLETON

Bitter rain barnstorms green's mean ark,
bringing a hairy eyeball to play on
the velocity of culture vultures, who talk
in offal accents of their new dreamland,
where it's the zeal of gods rolling their own
that is slapped down amidst hilliness,
ocean horizon's long grab at nothing.

Shearers wrestle sodden sheep off ute trays.
Lizards of steam climb the kitchen ceiling.
Lather's not strained as each glass is drained.
Choruses of bubbly streams traverse gullies
to echo the roar of a river's welcome,
while solitude of rain gangs up on all
gathered at Queen Tuatara's funeral.

Leaves
LORIN ELIZABETH

He makes her pancakes on school days,
uses half-empty cider bottles for pan oil and
flips them, like 10 cents every time your bed's made,
flips them like his golden syrup women,
a stack of unread newspapers
dusted with cinnamon.

On weekends, she escapes
busking for mauve pipis down the coast
where the galaxies are developed in a darkroom
star by star,
where campfires kick sparks against her shin and
foiled banana melts with chocolate and marshmallow.

She weaves a willow tree tiara to distract her hands
and whispers to the charred emptiness,
I'm leaving for a while.
Then she sends it in a text.

Phone in hand,
he smiles, dismissive and
swigs cider from the bottle,
pancakes for breakfast again.

Poem, interrupted

TIM EVANS

[To audience]
So I'm recovering from—

[Sound effect, phone buzzing]
DRRRING-DRRRING!
[Look down. Tap pockets]
DRRRING-DRRRING!

[Mime lifting phone to ear, right hand in 'phone' shape. Mumble, sigh.
    Look off to side]

Hello, who's this?
Oh, it's you.
The abyss.

Not the 1989 thriller directed by James Cameron?
Oh, [Nodding] the religious or philosophical concept of a deep, dark pit.
That one.

Yeah, I know. I've read Nietzsche.

Well, no.
Okay, the Wikipedia.
Well listen, I'm in the middle of something so—

you just want to catch up?
You got a message from depression?
[Aside] The shady fuck.

Yeah, I'm good thanks. Busy, busy
lots of work on. I'll start that eventually
no, not much going on socially
I'm still getting out occasionally
[Scratch head]
to see my GP, psychology, the pharmacy.

Well, yeah.
Depressingly empty.

But I've got really into thinking recently.
[Shrug shoulders] Yeah, you know, it's a hobby.
Well [Sigh] how to sum it up succinctly?
I guess life and its inherent futility,
contentment as an impossibility,
[Spread arm to side]
my insignificance in the dark of infinity.

[Drop arm]
That's why you're calling me?

I see.
Well I wouldn't call it staring into the abyss
more a glance, a peep, the occasional peek
just a quick poke around in the bottomless deep.

What?
Four hours today and most of last week?
[Spread arm to side] Well how do you … ?
[Drop arm and shoulders] You've been staring back?
[Shake head] Well I don't quite know what to do with that.

Yeah, yeah – still doing the poetry
yeah, still rhyming,
mostly.

[Look up] I'm on stage right now actually
[Look down] and it's a three minute limit.
Yeah it is kind of tight, so that's why I …

[Drop arm and shoulders]
Right.

[Shake head]
No I don't think they're laughing *at* me
it's the intersection of comedy and vulnerability.
Well I don't think it's pretentious and needy

[Hold up hand, palm facing out]
Look, the abyss, we've been through this already
[Point off to side]
I fought my demons deep in the beast's belly
and truly that was the battle that made me
but stay too long and the darkness negates me
[Point back to self]
I returned from inferno like Dante
anxiety become divine comedy.

[Hold up hand, palm facing out]
No, look, the abyss, well thanks for the invite
I'm sorry but I can't see you tonight
[Point down]
I'm in a place where art meets community
doing a thing called [Point in front] writing your own story
I think I might be finding some insight
illuminating darkness [Extend arm towards ceiling, palm open]
under this spotlight. [Bend arm back in towards head]

[Cover 'phone' with left hand. Look over to MC]

How am I doing for … ?
No?
[To audience]
No, that's it. That's time.

Vita means life

GABRIELLE EVERALL

After 'The Letters of Vita Sackville-West to Virginia Woolf'

Vita's present was death
she lived in the past
a knight
a fisherman
a motherfucker
to Lady Sackville
while she hauled in
Virginia Woolf
through a cold war
of telegrams
like a coke-whore
Virginia begs,
'Please just one more line'
a mistress of letters
ice-queen alphabets
bagging each other's
books and personality traits.

Vita plays
Mother Teresa
to Virginia's
leprous genius
who is
constantly sick
sick of everything
except Vita.

If one is
a dyke
one is
necessarily rogue
as difficult
and unpredictable

as a
nuclear warhead
as impenetrable
as the Amazon
and just as
unfuckable
a persistent man
who should be killed.

Vita raised
her blazing sword
was busy
slicing skulls and
excavating palaces
her arrogance
flattened armies
and civilizations
guided by
heavenly bodies
and men
bearing knives
she said, 'I'm off to
an endless year war
a discovery of
a new world
where I will become heir
and ambassador
to stateless love.'

Vita carves Persia
for her own
like the territory
of Virginia's heart
the first empire
there are at least
two types of booty
Virginia wears
a hieratic crown

emeralds run
through Vita's
hands and around
her stiff neck
pearls are emptied
from her shoes
blinded by diamonds.

Brushing with Tom
BELA FARKAS

Tom Cruise you're my hero and it's not because of your spectacular acting
    abilities
or because you walk around with that,
'I'm head of Scientology,' swag
or
'I've spent the last hour jumping on Oprah's couch,' swag.
Tom, I love your teeth, when your lips parade those wicked whites,
drool drips down my chin and into my beard.
Tom, I had a dream last night, that I was your dentist brushing your perfect
    ivories
with a small headed toothbrush and I knew what I was doing.
I brushed at a 45-degree angle against your gum line and using short back and
    forth strokes,
I brushed all chewing surfaces.
I brushed bristles on all 8 incisors, 4 canines, 8 premolars, 12 molars and 4
    wisdom teeth,
till they shined, shined so much that it was mission impossible to look at your
    beautiful
brown eyes when you spoke.
Then I whipped out the floss and snapped an 18-inch piece of that bad boy off
and glided it, glided it gently, carefully, between tooth and gum, I glided it in a
zig
zag
motion
until the plaque was annihilated and prayed that it never tried to inhabit such
    a perfect mouth.

Tom, I love your teeth.
Tom, I love your teeth.

Murmuration

JAYNE FENTON KEANE

You and I tangled and curled in each other
bodies camouflaged with bullet sized markings

the compass stills, then spins incessantly
in pursuit of a bearing that will sustain a hold

a scaffold, a loop, a return to base
a belief in being understood.

Words rest all over a heart.
Familiar and unnatural this breath

with its strong involuntary beat.
I feel you painfully close

eyes tuned to the inner frequency
of a moonless dark.

I watch you slip into breakage,
powerless, like watching smoke.

Couldn't identify the source.
I tried, covered in will, but

the end of a rainbow
is the colour of lit matches.

The body whose heart skips constantly
notices how ropes drop to the floor

as we undress, swallows high on voltage
flight lines detaching from magnetic guidance.

SCENIC MAPS PARTS

LIONEL FOGARTY

Merton VIC, 10.44 a.m., 2013-06-10

TAKE YOUR SMART PHONE AND RUSH
    A MIND TO ARTIST WAYS
TAKE YOUR IPADS AND FIND THE
PATHWAY THE BLACK MEN WALK AND TALKED BEFORE
THE DEVICES CONTENT DEMANDS.
INFATUATE IN DOWNLOAD OF A DREAMTIME REALITY LAYERS.
HAVE ALL RICH CLASSICS ON THOSE BLACKFELLAS KIDS
    WRITERS NOW,
MAN OF BOOKS ON GOINGS.
MAKE THE MOBILES UNITE A MEDIA TO GO TO OUR NEXT
    YEAR'S RIGHTS FIGHTS.
DO THE FAVOURITE EMERGING REALM OF LITERATURE OF
    EXPERIENCES.
DON'T FIELD THE WIZENED GHOST THAT EMBED FOR MONEY.
TAKE ALL IPADS AND PUT THEM IN THE OUTBACK STARS
    FALLING FOR THE FIRE LIGHTS.

To kill the Prime Minister
BENJAMIN FRATER

To kill the Prime Minister, organise a group of angry poets,
dress up in green rags and hover over his body.

To kill the Prime Minister, show him the wall crawling up a bug,
put him in a bright den to watch the lamb devour a lion –
he will require a change of clothes.

To kill the Prime Minister, rouse and provoke angry hermit farmers
to brandish ram-horn revolvers at the sky,
ready to take the sun!
To kill the Prime Minister,
 hit him with the shell-less tortoise of your mother's dream.

To kill the Prime Minister,
intolerably amplify through a wine bottle
the sound of your forbidden woman when you touched her starfish.
Tell the Prime Minister that you have also touched the starfish of his mistress.

To kill the Prime Minister, arrange a mafia in lime cheesecloth suits
to sing the national anthem sideways and kick the temples in.

To kill the Prime Minister,
bunch and present him with the terrorist flowers
forensics plucked from bombs delivered in antique suitcases.

To kill the Prime Minister, tell Wollongong University students
to slide into salamander skins and take to the trees!
With or without the wind, we will soar, saw and soar again.

To kill the Prime Minister,
lock him in the cupboard with the ravenous Moses.
To kill the Prime Minister, throw him headfirst into the moth pit.

To kill the Prime Minister, send him the eels of your bed
and giftbox the bird that stung your eye as the sun rose.
A Sun Rose is a very beautiful animal.
I would scale and eat you for it.

To kill the Prime Minister,
let him know that black-suited baboons
have deciphered the cabinet and escaped.
Let him know also that an old man with a long white beard
waits under a newspaper, prepared to eat his children
if he fails to deliver that Rubens painting to my caravan door by 3 a.m.

To kill the Prime Minister,
tie him up naked with seaweed to the apex of a driftwood triangle,
flog him with eel spines, slap him with stingray,
unzip and unleash the 50-year plague of hermit crabs.

To kill the Prime Minister, I will push my arm through the keyhole
and transmute from fist, to dove, to spider.

Reality on-demand
ZENOBIA FROST

1. Demo Day

Jo Gaines walks right into me and takes stock. *Good bones,*
y'all — I love this one. So much potential. Knuckle through a wall or two
and fill me up with light, hem back the big trees snagging eaves,
polish till you slide right off the slick of my boards. Tip out all my organs
and reset. Pull back my ceiling and truss me with fresh letter moulding.
A nest of bees released in a wall. The no-est house on Yes Street.
We just need the owner's original *mm* to do this right, to fold
the thumb in and open the kitchen right up with a pop.
May as well rebrand your favourite prime-time flippin' show
as *Fister Upher.* You're welcome. Chip is somewhere else making a joke
into the hollow of another episode. The revolution is caramelised
in Joanna's domestic vision. Let's play house. She leans in
to lick up her handiwork, like a bond cleaner — the deepest
just before she leaves. Furrows to hang a final pendant light
from my cervix. Gimme Carrera. If it feels too full, let's go low
on clutter. Are you ready to see your instant equity? Curbs
in all the right places. My muscles close around and vanish her work.
Any good renovation is invisible.

2. Nailed It
After Gertrude Stein

Plum caught up in a truffle. Butter burns uvula. Sage
crisps in a pan. The bruise of a poached quince
resurrects a collar. I can make my own pikelets. I can
live off you for weeks. Have we transcended turmeric?
A caramel slice forgotten in your fist. You can do just
about anything on granite, even real hot stuff. Put the
entire roast beetroot and its rose honey right there.

Layers of potato sunbathe in the oven. Fingers take a
dip in figs. A creamy void wakes in the blink of a
bagel. I'm not a morning person. A brain mornay. Roll
your forehead into the shortcrust. Melting moments
split the timer. A recipe is a letter to your body. And
your body is just a reply.

3. The Rose Ceremony

I am a dreadful flirt – the worst you've met.
She's come around to watch – is *this* a date? This ritual,
to narrate like Attenborough: here we see the men
in TV's natural habitat: The Mansion
set with daybeds, fairy lights, and ad breaks.
I want a rose more than I've ever craved a rose. Each bachelor
narrates, in turn, her entrance: *Sophie walks in wearing—*
and we're speechless. Adjectives are mislaid in the fracas.
I'm the one man in this blur of boys. What would they do
with all the cameras off? What would *we* do with cameras on?
It's like a bunch of pigeons with a chip. *Can I just grab you,*
Sophie, for a chat? (Does she even like *The Bachelorette*?)
The bachies pile their coats on Soph, till all we see
is bubbly flute and Uggs. You're probably warm enough,
so I won't offer. *When I want someone, I want it like a volcano.*
Sophie likes to sit on safe things only, like a couch.
This couch has not been safe for weeks – we even
tethered wi-fi from a phone once – so committed.
Our elbows keep making excuses. I learned to cook.
We know how to talk to girls, and how to date.
The female of the species picks off her lovers
one by one. *I know I'm not the typical Bachelorette.*

when they legalise gay marriage
FURY

when they legalise gay marriage i will push scrolls of poetic manifestoes
through the gloryholes at my local truck stop

when they legalise gay marriage i will personally tear up every marriage
certificate between heterosexuals and offer the pieces as confetti at my local kink club

when they legalise gay marriage i will propose to every one of my lovers
that they propose to every one of their lovers that they propose to every one of their lovers

when they legalise gay marriage i will put pipe bombs in the foundations
of every church, then call them and play 'It's Raining Men', 'Everybody Dance Now'
and 'Gimme! Gimme! Gimme! (A Man After Midnight)' down the phone to warn
them of their impending happiness

when they legalise gay marriage, pastors, bishops, cardinals, parishioners,
priests will all ask – what is the world coming to? i will tell them Beyoncé, techno
and Barry White.

when they legalise gay marriage i will surprise Tony Abbott with a male
stripper for his birthday. it will be a stripper dressed as Tony Abbott

when they legalise gay marriage, i will answer all the questions on my tax
forms with 'FINALLY'

when they legalise gay marriage i will totter down to the registry office
and apply for wedding permits for every pet i've had, alive or dead

82

when they legalise gay marriage i will buy an engagement ring that is
shaped like a dildo and propose to myself

when they legalise gay marriage i will send a letter every week to the
reigning PM about how marriage is a tax on the lonely

when they legalise gay marriage i will make a nuclear family
                                                    then detonate it

when they legalise gay marriage, airport security will only wave wands to
make wishes come true

when they legalise gay marriage, the queers on Nauru will be so grateful

when they legalise gay marriage, Pride's theme will be 'White'

when they legalise gay marriage thousands of straight people will tell me
to call it 'marriage equality'

    & i will hand them each a shit
    covered in glitter

Art, industry, architecture & pets

ANDREW GALAN

Six stories above, where I live
my stomach has moved on
I stare at postcard of what
in January, Picasso accepted.
This three up, three down, distinctly directed
ground-floor ziggurat to public relations
drags me backward, sometimes turning
never forward
across every boulevard
I hear as I go
the drone quack of Futurists and Marx.
It is six flights above where I hear the black sounds
Lorca is at the door. He twists at the knob.
But I lied about where I live.
I live on the ground floor.
It is six levels above, where I am headed
and I am dancing
spatial references which signal location,
newly installed frozen bulb with poison coil
bull and horse
their arrested market day screams
above pillars falling
away from high-rise
above gawkers
away from people
who speak and speak and speak as piston engines.
I lied, I am not dancing.
But I feel my legs tense
like Van Winkle running in place while reading.
How followable are you?
Is there a guide book?
Do you need that word?
Why is it 1937?

Don't write questions in poetry.
I lied. I am in bed wishing my dog would visit. Again I lied.
I don't have a dog. I have a cat.
This is a cat poem.

dog daze

IAN GIBBINS

as cool as marrowbone jelly | as hot as chocolate wax |
I have diamonds on my collar | sapphires and emeralds
ignite fire storms in my eyes ||

my skin is burnished bronze | I'm inked with ruby and quartz |
my braids are barbed wire slipknots |
cast-iron blades hackle my armour-plate spine ||

my nose tracks so close to ground | I can smell trouble
oozing up between the flagstones |
between the spreadeagled entrails | of your precious little conquests |
but who gives a flying fuck? | it's always about you ... ||

I can track the droplets of fear | the rank apprehension |
smirched between your toes | smeared beneath your slipshod heels |
as you search for safe retreat | amid the unexploded shells |
of your inglorious past ||

your friends in high places cannot help you now |
your rheumy Lord Mayors and pitch-forked company directors |
your billionaire bankers and bit-coin junkies |
will never lift a finger | to stem the shit storm |
building around your arse ||

because I am on to you | I've got your bases covered |
with nowhere to hide | you are out there on your own |
bare-boned on your long and solitary road ||

you see: I have the dirt | I have run the numbers |
your files will be deleted without a trace |
and only I can log you in | only I can authenticate your identity |
your pixelated captcha code | and only I will have the encryption key |

to your darkest imagination | your very worst nightmares |
as you skulk within your hypothetical corridors of power |
as you mindlessly warp your sense of priority : privilege : privacy |
as you fruitlessly bend your game plan to your inevitable defeat ||

under cover of darkness | you will not hear my footfall on rattling floorboards |
my breath fogging your double-glazed window panes |
I will be your back door man | your front door man |
your pit bull : your lone wolf | howling for restitution |
baying for repayment | of your festering debt |
and your mouldering IOUs ||

too late now to call for your doctor | that pain in your chest is yours for keeps |
but rest assured | be secure in the knowledge | I will be watching you |
and I have all the time in the world ||

yes: only one of us is counting | and I have diamonds to spare |
I have dog years | by the million |
I have dog years | to burn :||

Sedition – a letter to the writer from Meri Mangakāhia
ANAHERA GILDEA

Here's what I had in mind, kōtiro, this
clipping at words like overgrown maikuku –
return the blankets of domestic life; don't fold
washing or wear shoes, polish these rerenga kē.

Eh. But this world.
I s'pose neither of us planned to be in politics,
never did do what others told us to –
wahanui though, go on, get

your sedition on girl,
your agitator, your defiant speak
to each other eye to eye –
Māori been jailed for nouns, phrases;

butcher up a clause, get buried
in Pākehā kupu, then dig that
out like the old people. No one approved
of their language either.

Labels are for jars
MADDIE GODFREY

my dad is a mathematician
he raised me as a Venn diagram
called me half-boy, half-girl
we watched Quentin Tarantino
and *Tomb Raider*, he taught
me how to shave my legs
like he shaves his face

the day I got my hair cut short
he asked, *Do you still look like a girl?*
I think he hoped I would maintain
the mirror reflection that kept me the same
a souvenir of similarity that
aesthetically feminised me

I think my dad knew early
that I never suited a binary
so we acted as father and
son, puberty was not fun
I felt like my body betrayed
the censored secrets I fled
you can't be a Venn diagram
once you start to bleed

instead, I was two fractions
which could not be made complete

I was the space within a failed high-five
where two palms do not meet

if binary was a bathtub
my limbs were too lanky
to fit inside

so like a high school
graph, I used colours to
distract and hide

I was taught you can't bend gender
it is ruled lines on graph paper
traced with permanent marker
and so I was marked as Her
as Female, Woman, She
but these labels were hand-me-downs
that never quite fit me

I have never felt trapped
in my body, only trapped by
what others expect from it
I have never been ashamed
of my breasts, only of
what they signify
these flesh mounds tell tales
can never keep a secret safe

gender fluidity is not an equation, or a solution
it is the page number that remains un-notable
until you need to make a reference

my dad is no longer a mathematician
but he still loves me as a Venn diagram
accepts the space where two circles combine
as Lara Croft, as Tarantino
both at the same time

Brookside bramble
HADLEY

And the sun comes up like a red, wet fist, and sets
the brook to bake with that sweet smell of dust and decay.

And the algae clings to the brook-bed like a tenacious
bad idea, and the clay dyes the water the colour of horse
diarrhoea, and the cicadas buzz like cicadas.

And this bit of driftwood looks like an elephant skull,
and rusty pliers are close as we come to dinosaur bones,
and a kookaburra smashes an old bong-hose headfirst into a rock.

And the brookside sandbanks are covered with tin cans and smashed glass,
and I keep having the dream where I put them in my mouth.

And the gum tree bark peels off. It's got cirrhosis of the liver.

And this short cliff-face of shale and dead hay looks like an old man
trying to catch the bus, with a terrible haircut.

And the lizards are curling out the sides of these crossroads,
licking the air like bible salesmen. When you spook them,
they raise up, and freeze. Look at them freeze.

They look like headstones. Like a strange, mobile cemetery of scales
that marches closer every time you look away. And—

hey! is that a dead eel floating downstream, or a man's arm waving?
hey! is that a plastic bag trapped in the rocks, or a man's face smiling?
hey! is that a shoal of catfish chasing water bugs, or a man's heart beating?

hey, am I standing on this bridge, or have I drowned already?

And I see caterpillars dancing, in the far-too-green grass, and a closer look
    reveals they're covered in black ants.

And there's so many folks who dance,
dance and wave their arms to distract from the fact they're being eaten alive.

It's why cancer is so popular, because it's some death you can fight.

And the cobra on the path ahead may be a butterfly, but the hole
in the ground they'll stow you in, is always right behind.

Stuff

DAVID HALLETT

Bluetooth Blu-ray Myspace YouTube
megabyte terabyte HDTV
email eBay iPod MyPod
CD LCD DVD … 3D
… download … download,,,
website War Games Xbox airbags
high-speed broadband hands-free Dolby
foxtel facebook cellphone ringtone
MP3 PS3 Telstra-Optus PSP
more for me /more for me/ more for me/ more for me!
Google & cable GPS ABS
Interest-free/ payment-free
till 20-20-23 … plus
a motion-sensor-game-console-brangelina-Barbie-doll …
with cruise control …
cash or card?
savings, cheque or credit?
Twitter-Twitter-tweet-tweet-Twitter
blog!

Ham and cheese toasties

JORDAN HAMEL

Every day something disappears,
I'm never sure what it is.
A chair, some drawers, our repertoire,
a night we camped out on the roof,
stitching together our last desperate dawn
with contempt for the plans others make.

There's no more need for that toastie machine,
bought with change seeking refuge in the creases Trade Me couches make.
We've sacrificed bread to the gods of gastric distress
and the rusted amber handle, with congealed Edam icicles
was graceful in its abandonment.
Postmodernism never fooled this little press
into delusions of George Foreman-esque grandeur.

I've never understood grief or masculinity.
How long should touch linger in these final moments?
Slap my ass, make a joke.
It's hard to have resolve sometimes.
Like crying all night in the bathroom of a corporate function
and calling it *networking*.
Or a kindergarten teacher, shitting himself in front of the children out of
    solidarity.

One day we'll build our own commune,
in the hills Te Aro keeps for itself.
We'll meditate on lost friendships.
There will be no young fanatics,
only a cautionary tale.
Old men with stiff backs, soft cocks and failed plans to spread Marxism.
The hymns will be My Chemical Romance
and the Kool-Aid will be a cask of Country Red.

Customs: a love story

MOHAMED HASSAN

Dear Airport Customs Officer,

I know you want me.

I saw you staring from across the terminal. That dark look in your eyes.
A hunger you don't quite understand.

Maybe it's the way my name swirls around your tongue. My olive skin.
My piercing eyes on the grainy passport photo.

You tell me it's random, but I know. The moment our eyes locked,
you couldn't wait to get your hands on me.

Strip me down. Search through my baggage.
I don't have much but I'll share it with you.

I'm not saying I ain't flattered. Getting chosen out of all these people.
Watching their jealous sneers as I'm lead down the aisle and into the
    questioning room.
Cold seats and harsh lights. It's the way I always dreamed it would be.

And you have so many questions. Where I grew up? Am I single?
Have I ever been part of an international terrorist syndicate?

This is all moving so fast!

Listen. Let's take things slow. I want this, I do, but let's build a relationship
on more than just racial profiling. I want you to know the real me.

Can't you see that I,
Well …

I'm just a boy, standing in front of a boy
asking him to let me in.

How to stay afloat
KELLY LEE HICKEY

It goes like this.

You take some small part of yourself,
fashion it into a paper boat.

Be careful with the delicate folds,
ensure it is water tight.

Just below the bow
blow your wish.

Carry it gently.

Under no circumstances
should you try to put it in your pocket.

In your hands is the only safe place.
Keep your palms open at all times.

When you come to the water,
do not jump in.

This is why you built a vessel.

You are a land-dwelling mammal
all hot blood and need for oxygen.

The wind licking sails is not the same
as breathing.

Get down low.

Not in prayer, but for practicality
you want to see this close up,

test the wind with your saliva
streaked across one finger,

it's not fail proof, every assumption
is based in some part on a lie.

Now gather your breath
your bellowing mammalian weakness,

poise the boat against the water,
the boat against your lips.

Draw back the wind like an arrow,
hold it like grudge.

Take this small fragment of yourself
floating. Let it go and don't look back.

Hotel room
DOMINIC HOEY

On the 14th floor we are dressed as the best versions of ourselves
somebody's died in here you can feel it
you're high off some garbage
sitting in a spa bath spewing laughter
talking about how we need education and better drugs
rewriting our lives
with words stolen from some Hollywood fantasy
you saw on an airplane once

we're the same person me and you
just the opposite sex
wrapped in faded tattoos and neon pain
sharing secrets for a cheap high
cos everything is like shitty porn

after the fact we lie in our filth
you read a book called *Love is Submission*
outside morning crawls up the stairs
between its impossibly white teeth
hangs a world where we are
sons and daughters
workers
victims
lovers

and I would stay here with you
living off room service until cancer
but my credit is a memento
from a character building summer
and the only change in my pockets comes in 50 milligrams
and you need 4 to really make the sediment dance

a vacuum cleaner yawns in the distance
we get dressed in last night
and stumble out of here
smiling like we're too stupid to know how this ends

When women go to war
ELEANOR JACKSON

It will not be pretty. Much as you might like
to think we would bring a feminine touch.
It may seem strange, but we have trained in trenches

just as terrorist as theirs: the birth, the bed, the brothel.
These were the places where we were the spoils
of war. We are as capable of cruelty as men.

When the time comes, each woman will leave
the field, the factory, the suburban noose that comforts,
and at the appointed hour, solemn as the coming drum

taking every girl child with us, we will start walking
to the desert, to the forest, to the bush.
No food or water, resting never, not until

there is a swathe of bodies laid out along each road,
every mewling baby quiet, until the air is still as doom.
Ending life at last, as men have longed to do.

Nostromo
JOELISTICS

1.

The streets are empty as shit and we just ride em like ghosts
in the place where we live we've got nowhere to go
pushbikes on the road we take flight with the crows
the night sky above and tarmac below us.
The city lights are majestic off in the distance
over the rooftops we float.
Above the dreams of a suburban night
we snuck out while my parents slept to take a ride and we,
we ride our bikes to the bay and take a walk on the wharf
sit on the edge and light a ciggie like a torch.
You turn and you talk to me I'm looking away
I'm listening to every single thing that you say
you say, The future's bright man, tomorrow is ours
and there will come a day soon when we leave this town
the clouds they start to gather so we get up and leave
and we're home before the dawn even touches the trees.

2.

We always said that these suburbs were like a cemetery
you always said you'd escape that's what you said to me.
You got away not in the way that you thought
and now I walk along old tracks and I'm looking for yours.
And in the middle of similar looking scenes
as I step off from the gutter and gather the things I need
midnight's light makes life look lifelike
the antenna's and tennis courts
this town is menopause.
I know my way around and I could play it down
the streets are like the back of my hand
and memories abound.
But now it's different, I'm different the difference is that I visit
I don't stick around, I don't even miss it.

I get a vision of a version of my high school days
most weekends you would spend at my place
and your face is in these streets, it haunts me now
that's why I struggle when I head homebound.

3.

You always had your own rhythm to keep the comedy coming
you were as close as a brother man I think of you often
how you talked with a passion, how you rationed your cash
you stood six foot tall above the rats.
You had a habit of thinking you were the smartest motherfucker in the room
and it was generally true
on the real you were a hero, a friend of the highest order
a companion when the girls that we chased were all we thought of.
Whoever you are wherever you're from
we all get given time and then it's time to move on
one day you're in the midst of it, the next you're gone
and if you think it's different to that you're wrong.
Life's an addiction we're all on the nod
and it's a beautiful dream so dreamer dream on
breathe in, remember everything from the start
the end is the beginning the beginning is past.

Girls like me

TERI LOUISE KELLY

get to die every day
get spat at shat on
jeered & ridiculed –
for daring to be
alive: Girls like me
in this world full of hypocrisy
pimp their own buns
in red-light districts
just to make it to
the promised
land: Girls like me get
to ride all the rides
for half the recommended
retail price.

Mosque
ZOHAB ZEE KHAN

Come,
enter our Mosque.

Come inside and you'll find no monsters reside here.
Mind clear
when head to the ground
no sound
Mosques be *lifely* silent
I just find this the best place to find
                    peace/s
                        of puzzles
                            just fit better when here.
we no longer bedouin cameleers
we now doctors, lawyers, engineers
we now poets, CEOs and comedians
they say we be in
            dark days
            mind haze
but when I enter the Mosque
            prostrate
    I find clearer pathways.
We say
Assalamu'alaikum warahmatullahi wabarakatuh
at least ten times a day
aka
may the peace and blessings of God be upon you
you
know not peace
till you stare at majestic scrawl calligraphy atop domes
Mosques be resting places for travelling souls
our minarets our lighthouses calling us home
call me your brother
for we were never meant to travel this life thing alone.

One little lonely moment on the train from Brisbane to the coast, and just like that
SIMON KINDT

I am back on the train to Mount Kōya
watching an old man at the station,
tending to the little gas lamp flames
that keep the points from freezing shut
while behind him, another man pulls branches
from the drying stack outside the shed, sings
and stokes the stove that keeps them both
from freezing in the air.
And here we are again —
hands sifting through a language
to describe two men tending to their fires
while I think about a cedar tree —
how it holds the fall of snow
and how a history is written in its rings.

Is there a name for the sound of snow
descending through the still?
Or the way a trail cut into a hill insists,
even as it fades and disappears, on being
followed?

I think I have spent a great deal of this life looking
for ways to leave the body.

For example,
I can walk until this trail disappears into the snow,
look up to cedars reaching up like prayers
and keep on walking

or,
I can think of an old man at a train station
breaking branches for the fire,
hear them cracking into splinters,
and imagine writing on my ribs

the noun for snowflakes snagged
on cedar branches
as the man breaks prayers between his hands
and sings them to the air.

Finger on the map
LANIYUK

Finger on the map
This is mine now
Flag on the hill
It's the Union Jack
Invading the red
The yellow
And the black

That attempt on genocide
Never did subside
They're busy
Filling the minds of black and white
With lies
'Hey you mob,
Let's Recognise'
Fuck that shit
Let's Decolonise
Let's reprogram our minds
And realise
That we're all still slaves
Slaves to a system that took the children away
Raped the women as their men lay in pools of blood
Oh no wait!
Hold up
Slaves to a system that TAKES our children away
RAPES our women as our men sway by ropes

A powerful people but we weren't ready
Ready for a king that lacked integrity
Ready for sickness and guns and big cities
Ready to battle a man that didn't fight hand to hand
But with poison and bullets and prisons
FUCK THIS SYSTEM
Imperialism came by boat
Then infiltrated our minds

Arrived with the bible, a forked tongue and a bottle of wine
No need to kill us when you're keeping us institutionalised
Now they're turning our suffering into dollar signs
Turning our forest and our desert into uranium mines

Meanwhile we're lowering our Elders into early graves
Leaning in to kiss the soft greys of their heads
Only to turn around to bury our cousins next

Tonight we stand on unrelinquished land
Knowing always
That our Sovereignty
Was never ceded

And Resistance
Never ended

#commute
KLARE LANSON

The line we see between country and city
is a Kurt Vonagurt novel, it's a V.
It moves from our breakfast or lack thereof
our packed bags, our coffee queue
our swiping tickets; we are valid, we are
changing from horizontal to vertical.
The landscape blurs and within
the frame of the train is a painting.
We drink quietly, this composition of local colour;
gathering thoughts, shaping them, fragments of self.
It is dark. It is grey. It is vaguely blue.

As we speed through country it's all hard class here.
The familiar breeds nonchalance.
We are calm, we are casual but
if anyone sits in our seat we will turn.
We are in pairs yet we are alone. We tap tap tap
tap tap tap and then we become uneasy
because we have forgotten something.
We will never know what it is.
We will always know what it is.
Streaks of colour towards gunmetal roads.
Farmlands turn into dollhouse suburbs, where
the electrical wires move in waves, weird and fluid.
They rest sometimes on cowboy towers, guns at the holster.
Stolen land for the sake of connection.

The speed changes and we lose our place in time.
Skyline contracts as we move towards our destination.
Reflections show sleeping faces;
heads down, nostrils flaring, nodding in our
most private, most vulnerable.
We fall in love and our hearts are broken, all in one sitting.
We need something in our hands to fill the void.
A book. A newspaper. A mobile device.

The laptop. We logon, check our status tap tap tap
think about what we'll have for dinner.

How many times have you quit your job on this journey?
Walked towards your nearest dream, purchased flowers?
How many times does this journey press against you?
Would you like one of my mints?
We like to get on the Quiet carriage because
our stories are worn out by repetition.
As we slow down we become the whip that ripples
as it flicks into action.
We stepped on at the end so we could arrive at the beginning.
It's very clever; a calculated risk.
We are hyper mobile and we're walking in a circle,
patterns that generate motion to bring us home.

Whakamana
DAISY LAVEA-TIMO

W-h-a-k-a-m-a-n-a- spells Whakamana
It's the indigenous Māori word for empowerment
I found Whakamana at my local footy club

Beautiful bone crusher
She's the upward, outward and future facing
CEO of the heavy hitters club

See jerseys 6 & 7?
They're the multilingual and strategic playmakers
Who pūkana the rugby ball from any corner of the field

She's all about the fundamentals

Wairuatanga – the spiritual
+
Whānaunatanga – the relationships
+
Kōtahitanga – collective action
=
Bridging our systemic silos

E hara taku toa i te toa takitahi, he toa takitini
Because a champion team will always beat a team of champions, right?

Whakamana is jazz music
Agile in thought and creativity she scats through the defence
Agile in action she's the Bull running it straight up the middle
Her synergy so in the pocket
She sprints onto a floating ball
#Where'sTheOne?

Whakamana eats burpees for breakfast
Broncos for lunch and
F45 Papanui for dinner

Up, down, back 10m for the whole 80 minutes
When I want to give up
Whakamana kneels at the altar
Where capitalism and activism collide
And whispers Rhimes through her Nike megaphone
'Daisy ask not if your dreams are crazy
                    But *are they crazy enough?*'

Sis, keep pushing to that dark place
Juxtaposed there is the light,
the flow, the hum
In the hum you can see the marathon finish line
In the hum you're marshalling troops into formation
and you are Beyoncé
All at the same time!

Whakamana is altruistic leaving no man, woman or child in need of a
    cultural home
Her kaupapa?
Be kind
Be kind
Be kind

Whakamana's K-tape, sock tape and 3D tape mummified body
Shows up every week
I quickly learn
Effort and Respect
are the only currencies that matter here
In this rugby league arena,
Whakamana's actions give me evidence
of my own potential
These Mana Wāhine
Playwrights of power
Gladiators if you will
Continue to allow me to borrow their bravery
And wear their bigger shoes
With which to leave deeper prints

She's the Jacinda to my Chlöe
And the Ciara to my Parris Goebel
And it's time to Level Up

W-h-a-k-a-m-a-n-a- spells Whakamana
It's the indigenous Māori word for empowerment
I found Whakamana at my local footy club

The wheel

MICHELLE LAW

We're shown to a table inside,
where the lights from the wheel bear down on us.
It's balmy and tourists have sought refuge in the carriages,
secured and sky-high already —
or on the ground, poking around in their waist wallets,
scrounging for money, holding bills up to the light,
trying to make sense of this foreign currency.

No locals we know have set foot on the wheel,
except for my older brother.
He hopped on one afternoon with work colleagues and
spent the whole time on his phone.
There was a voice in the booth that told riders
Inspector Gadget 2 was filmed in the area.
See the iconic South Bank walkway covered in flowering vines?
Look familiar? Like you might have seen it on the big screen before?
Not even the original film.
He was ready to get off after one rotation but the wheel kept turning.

The waiter for our table tells me I look
Stunning tonight.
You don't hear him, so I repeat what he said.
The waiter is gay, has been checking men out all night,
wants a good tip, but he still noticed.
I wait for you to say something but you just smile and say,
That's nice.
You're quiet at dinner because we're at a big table with my family
and noise overwhelms you.
Not the sound of cutlery striking crockery,
nor shrieking laughter, but the conversation —
the effort it takes to be heard above it all.

You hate being out of control,
dining out at new places,
being surrounded by too many people.

You rarely go out, but tonight you've made a concession.
It's my birthday.
Say that I look nice, that you want me.
The wheel keeps turning.
Tourists enter carriages. They take selfies on their phones.
They're bored by the third rotation, pretend to enjoy themselves,
like the eighteen dollars they've spent is worth it,
that this ride is a memory they'll cherish.
They've paid a lot, made a commitment.
When is it time to get off?

Months later, I am in my brother's car, driving alongside the river.
We notice the wheel is gone.
My sister and I are in the back seat. I ask,
Where did it go?
They've taken it for maintenance, for cleaning,
left a big, open nothingness in its place.
Only a patch of darkness now, dim lights reflecting off the
sandy walls of the concert hall and onto the water.
I think of you, avoid thinking of you,
I try to remember how tall you are when you're standing beside me,
and what your voice sounds like.
How we are still friends,
have only been friends for so long.
When is it time to get off?

Yiayia
LUKA LESSON

My Grandmother
grew up between two wars in Greece
lost her brother Christo to the Germans
and named my mother Christina after him

Rare for a Greek woman, she had a divorce at fifty
and has lived for thirty years by herself
with his photos still in the spare room
she is a green thumb

She makes cordial from her own mandarins
drinks tea from her own chamomile bush
and picks tomatoes from her garden whenever I say I feel like a
σαλάτα
she hardly went to school

But one day
when talking of my time at University
and admiring all three different types of basil she has
growing in her garden
she says to me:
'Luka, eat two leaves basil every day
good for the blood
good for the brain
they don't teach that University'

And when my brother Eliah says to her:
'You know Yiayia
– you know a lot; you're really smart ...'
She always replies:
'Yees Eliah, I'm a very education.'

So recently I decided to ask my Yiayia
what she thought about racism
and whether it was okay for Greeks to still hate the Turks

for what they did to us in the past
and she said:
'Racism? No.
Just because some people naughty, doesn't mean you throw
the rest in the rubbish.'
Her name is Katerina Batounas
but her maiden name is Sarandavga.
And Sarandavga
literally means 'forty eggs'
and as the story goes
one of her great-grandfathers
was challenged by another villager
to see if he could eat an omelette made entirely with forty eggs
without getting sick

And anyone that knows my appetite
will know that I'm proud to say
he won that bet
and so his nickname 'Forty Eggs'
then turned into the family name
and was passed down the generations
to my Yiayia
and today
it's her birthday
so I tell her what we always do
Να εκατοστήσεις
'May you live to one hundred'
but she is 83
so instead of thanking me she says:
'Oh God me!!
A hundred??!!
No thank you, I have enough
maybe couple more years – then I go to sleep'

Where will you go to sleep Yiayia?
'In the cemetery – I already buy a "lili" house there …
I don't afraid!!'

Until then
she will keep calling me to see if I am too cold when I'm
visiting Melbourne
keep stopping me from doing the dishes
after she cooks us a meal
keep trying to slip me a fifty dollar note
every time I visit
and keep telling me:
'Eat two leaves basil everyday
good for the blood
good for the brain'

They don't teach you that
at University.

The LION Speaks
L-FRESH THE LION

Don't mistake patience for waiting.
The lion doesn't wait.

It strikes when the time is right.
When it can sense fear in the air
and when silence says more than words.

It watches closely from a distance
observing every move,
patiently.

It understands that every second is a minute
and that every inch is a kilometre.
Each precise movement is calculated.

Predestined.

Its launching stride is unexpected,
but it is the culmination of years
spent learning the intricacies of the art;
having spent time in the shadows
wanting so desperately to venture out
into the darkness.

Its strike is powerful.

And its voice is an echoing statement
that lets the world know that its time is now.

Don't mistake patience for waiting.
The lion doesn't wait.

Somehow fragile

ELEANOR MALBON

I remember the shape of my father's arm
reaching for a sail on the rented catamaran
I watched his shoulders squeeze together
as he thought about jumping
from the boat into the ocean
the sun sent shadows from his muscles
and he looked
strong to me
before the ocean
as only a father can

and then in next wave breath
he was somehow fragile
a small figure on the edge of the civilized zone
where the buildings cannot push
where the suits cannot step
and he looked
tiny to me
before the ocean
as only a father can

My Australia
SARA MANSOUR

When people ask me where I'm from
I tell 'em Punchbowl
More often than not, they smile, and reply
'No, where are you FROM?'
I sigh, roll my eyes and in an explanatory tone respond
PUNCHBOWL
You know ... it's near Bankstown
The city where mouths do not ebb the flows of
'Welcome' in over 60 different tongues
Where over 100 nationalities are housed under one postcode
This is my ode to the only place I know
Where one is told to go back
Because everyone understands
This is my ode to home

My Australia is
Walking through the streets of Punchbowl
With the smell of freshly roasted Lebanese coffee kissing
The Asian bakeries good morning
The eucalyptus towers overhead and the frangipanis scent my breath
As we sing the unofficial national anthem
'I come from a land down unda ...'
Living from beat to beat
Bumping down the streets
With Tupac on our tongues and
We're headed for the beach
Water, so unapologetically salty to the eyes
But we take it in our stride
Remembering all the lessons at Greenacre pools and at school
When Cronulla hit high tide
My Australia is barbecues
Or as my dad still says, 'BAR-BEE-KU'
Meat sizzling on the fire
Homemade tabouli and tomato sauce
Pavlova cake and knafeh

The perfect cultural dichotomy and it's not hard to see
No matter our creed
We always rep our team
#WanderersFC

This country
Will never be tainted by café sieges
We will always ride together
From the mountains where the bushfires rage
We stand together
Down to the shore where the lifesavers age
Under that great Southern Sun

My Australia is one
Where women wear their saris and their colourful hijabs proudly
Men don sweat-stained collars like war badges
You can get the best pho in Sydney
The realest Lebanese and Chinese
And you feel at ease because no one judges your garlic breath or the
Tabouli stuck in your teeth
It is finding the most authentic spices
In shops where signs in foreign languages
Sit like jewelled crowns atop their doors
It is neighbours passing barbecued meat over the fence
And always saying hello
It is all the stoic traditions
It is stoic – a community that's been hardened by media headlines
It is targeted
It is judged
It is 3 a.m. sirens and perceived thugs

But it is also where the calls to prayer
Gently interlude with the ringing of church bells
It is co-existence
And artistic resistance
Like the 4elements Youth Hiphop Festival
And the largest poetry slam in the country

It is my dad's voice 25 years on
Accent thick with resilience
Warm like an autumn sun
Smelling of petrol and truck smoke and all the forgotten things
All the zataar and the tahini and the crushed petals that were once dreams
Saying
We are lucky
It's not perfect
But it's home
It will never be perfect, but it will always be home
Home. When the rest of the world says no.

Pussy cat
SELINA TUSITALA MARSH

Pussy cat, pussy cat
Where have you been?
I've been to London
to visit the Queen.

Pussy cat, pussy cat
What did you there?
I frightened the western world
with my big hair

My moana blue Mena
My Plantation House shawl
My paua orb
My Niu Ziland drawl
My siva Samoa hands
My blood red lips
My Va philosophising
My poetic brown hips

Then standing before Her Majesty
And the Duke of Edinburgh
Centered Polynesian navigation
Ensuring I was thorough
In proposing a timeline
Subverting West is Best
Instead, drawing a circle
Encompassing all the rest

Houso kid

LAURIE MAY

I'm a pale mixed race
Product of a broken home
Raised by a single mother
Government housing estate kid
So go on
And judge me

So don't expect me to share your misguided notions
Of family based in broken religion
Raised by government views
Swallowing force fed convictions
Because I –
Am intellectual violence
Assaulting bogan mentality with straightforward non-physical brutality

A fan of non-physical resistance
A child of protest
But no freedom songs have I sung here
Struggling with every step here
This, mate this, is poverty here
So go on
And judge me

I am progeny of empty promises
And empty dreams
Bruised egos and black eyes
But never will I share your views of low class
No class
Shoeless trash

It's a compromising you've got yourselves in
Filled with hate and miseducation
But yeah it's us with the problem
Us houso kids
With our wide eyes

And tired sighs
Our open thighs
And our get-rich-quick schemes
Our deft fingers that quickly nick and flick up
Lowering the price of your investments with our tatty clothes
And lack of direction
And dreams
For a better life
Yeah it's us with the problem
Fighting against corruption
Bureaucracy
Against poverty
STDs
Redundancies
Policies
And the suffocating CLP

We're not concerned with your investments
We're just worried about where the rest went
Not concerned with your portfolio
Because you know, the closest thing to a portfolio
Any of us ever got
Was a sketchbook
Full of song lyrics and tattoo designs

And even though I'm now university educated
Grammatically correct
Pose with elegance not ignorance
Filled with love and notions of unity
At the end of the day
To you
Yeah
I'm still just a houso kid
So go on
Judge me

Spree
IAN McBRYDE

Earlier today.
  First reports put.
    Among the dead are.
      Informed sources say.
        No one was present when.
          There are no witnesses who.
            Authorities are puzzled as to.
              Detectives wish to question.
                Family members deny any.
              Neighbours said he never.
            The late edition features.
          The police are seeking.
        It is now hoped that.
      New leads indicate.
    Survivors are.
  The suspect.
Fresh.

Val Plumwood canoe

LAURA JEAN McKAY

The Master knows that
dogs are clocks and women
clocks with mops and locks
and even though we keep time – we tick,
we tick,
we keep it –
that's Master's name there on the door.

Past rings of sun-warmed sediment –
a breathless fridge.
Master doesn't know about it. Or
the longboat made from wood.

The pot plant upends
before we can look to water.

It's a response.
The dirt
is dead.
The plant, the water, the nails that scrape it from the floor.
A machine can't die, dear,
darling, disparate, dove.
Dirt doesn't die
(but time bends in water).

The machine that lusts,
dances on the wall.
We feel a kinship with her flat face and embarrassing bodily noises.
She can't stop shouting the hour!

Hello sailor.
Hello pizza guy.
Hello Liza.
Our bodies puckered sundials. We puked up the rest.
Hello nature.

Hello nurture.
Hello Master, it's midnight.

Master is very still on the clean pillowcase
bleached
but still breathing
(we tick too
we tick for you).
Master is watching
our pallid legs and how
they skim the jaw.
He's everywhere and nowhere while
we bleed old babies over sheets.
Is that you, Master?

Legover window and fence –
the tidemark grunts and growls.
A creature is awake down there:
gnarled and woody reptile,
fallen tree.
A jaw lined with teeth,
gaze trained.
Liza.

We share a name, dear.
We share a
longboat made from wood.
We've leaned too far.
Seen interest bloom in the animal I.
Time drops into the estuary, where it
rolls like rocks.

In the death roll there is a burnt-chop formality,
an intimacy of teeth.
Bubbles laugh around us. Smokey
blood,
plays a catchy tune.

Master knows a thing about the universe
and how to hold a gun.
He pisses on the lemon tree
because nitrogen feeds the machine,
makes lemons, dogs and how your little girls grow.
Checks his phone.
There's something on at seven,
eight, nine and ten.

A hole in the bucket
(oh dear)
invites water.
We drag from each other through the churning.

Master has two cigarettes.
He lights one
for the other.
Liza.
Shakes his head.

We tick for you.

No motorbikes, no golf
COURTNEY SINA MEREDITH

Way South
I said where you from baby?
And you said Way South

Nup
nah
never been there
what grows there
women or moss?

And you said
Way South flowers
purple hearts with blood grape trim and hymns

hymns like cotton fish across the white sun
a smoky cherub wide-eyed chorus

wailing on and calling on
and falling on
hymns

rise up from the baking tar
a rose cloud of voice

a crimson Cortina on the corner
and Lorna is a nice name for a girl
and Paola is a nice name for a black Tahitian pearl
hymns

rise up from the shadow limbs
and yard milk sodden mouth

out the back round the back
down the back

and you said
Way South.

It isn't like an Island nipple nup
no breezing trees and caramel sand
no coconut truths spilling over woven fans
no plans of making love to the land.

There isn't a wooden face
to stand my hands against and still

the rising falling chest
the salty dusky mess
Way South like a bat back to hell.

Babies grow in babies
leaving paisley prints on ladies' skin

finer than and greener than
a pounamu teardrop
in the eyes of no-man's-land.

But can you hear the voices?
Clear as chimes at dusk
we eat sea hearts
black and pulsing
skin the shells of
silver rust
this is where
the angels come
to down their wings and cuss!

'Way South'
like dead love
walking
wailing
crawling
back to lust.

You can spy
the timber spine
of every creature
on his step

straight for cemeteries resting heads
and flower beds on top of death beds

joking 'bout the big smoke
and the doubts that will not rest

souls pity the metal facts of the city
nodding that we've missed
the dunes and cliffs

lining pebbles skyward
gift upon gift
the mountain body
stands and lies
Way South
where the beast sleeps
Way South
with its mean streets
and ciggie stained teeth.

Nup
nah
I've never been there,
what grows there?

Way South
Way South.

Night's knows

MILES MERRILL

If Night had a nose
of course it would be running
from the bridge on down.
Night's thick calves would cha-cha-cha
holes in your dance floor.
It's hair? Black fire; under control
but still dangerous.
Night's face: Venus in the open sky,
a mask over back alleys wet with trash.
But the eyes are green flashing lights saying, 'Go-go-go-go ...'
Night's body of course would be heavenly
with little needle holes to let the stars shine through.
If night were me, I'd kill the sun and never let you go.
– Beats like a big bass drum –
– Moans like scotch pouring through a saxophone –
Night's lips would always be pouting and puckered on some cheap sick
    movie star.
It's voice a ka'billion cars
RevRevRevvvving with alarm.
I tell you It breathes
sweet magnolia breeze.
When morning comes creeping in that back door
and all sane people are asleep,
there's just me and you
playing in the abandoned puddles of dawn.

Rooftops in Karachi
MISBAH

My cousin has named all of his homing pigeons. He takes them in his soft hands and feeds them, but I have a feeling he could just as easily use those hands to snap their thin necks. My other cousin who lives in the same house goes around shooting cats. Since I arrived I have been putting out bowls of milk each night. Another cousin has an imaginary lover who she has introduced me to. She makes him out to be so real that I believe he is. But I can never seem to see him, which is not due to him being imaginary but because he is shy and agile. She describes the way he kisses her, and the conversations they have, and to this day I remember his name. I know it's been said that falconers feel their hearts soar with their falcons, but I don't think it's just a feeling.

types of men
SCOTT-PATRICK MITCHELL

there are men who treat
privilege as a begging bowl,
bodies as 'participation' trophies,
for whom revenge is pornography
& entitlement a sweat-stained cap
turned backward

you are not such a man

some men are an ungentle
juggernaut, jagged against
silk, a throat full of fists,
dried blood the colour of
their love, scabs licking
knuckles, bones replaced
with alcohol

you are not such a man

it's not them i fear, it's their smell:
                aggression
                dirty socks
                shit-talking
                forced sex

these men smell of bad childhoods,
worse decisions &
so many repressed emotions

we need men who smell like
tenderness, boundaries, hope,
flowers

we need men
who smell like
                you

Hipster killer
MORGANICS (FEATURING CORE RHYTHM, HYJAK AND DJ MK-1)

'Do you like my new iPhone case? It's made out of macadamia nuts, it's soooo awesome.'
'I'll have a rice milk decaf mocha, weak on the chocolate, extra hot, in a cup to go, thanks.'
Now, I'm in a hurry so can you make it fast, my fixie is unlocked and I just don't trust that homeless guy out front.'

I can feel it in the air tonight, there's a reason for this rhythm and it's getting me hype,
there's a mission that I gotta complete, no defeat, there's people acting stupid and they're roaming the street.
Bare feet, old leather shoes, lost their socks, ride around on a fixie but don't have a lock.
Can't afford a razor but they sure pay a lot for their vintage clothes from the right clothes spot.
'I'm a rockabilly bushranger bag lady!' Ha, you don't know shit and you drive me crazy.
Busy reminiscing for a time you never knew, pre–civil rights, pre-feminism too.
Now their girlfriend rocks their grandma's clothes, it looks like they're homeless so how can you know
that they don't own a yacht when they wear boat shoes, they gentrify neighbourhoods
and play the blues.

Who am I?
I'm a Hipster Killer!

136

Daily bird parasite, locust on the plains, Einstein Sherpa swastika on your chain
urban outfitted with premade stains, rockin' a fro-hawk with He-man Haynes
slave chain fix trace make it emo, occupy, occupy, one per cent you're a zero
all the talk about I remind you of Don Cheadle,
spike your echinacea, poison your frappucino
'I love black people', you're talking some Tarantino
slow your roll, get animated like *Finding Nemo*,
damn culture vultures, I'm playing Captain Repo
taking this back 'cause you'll never be my equal
Real McCoy boy, said y'all are weapon lethal
cool hak or G-star, smooth, can't repeat
take your JT back to some other street
and cut the false bop 'cause you'll never find the beat!

Who am I?
I'm a Hipster Killer!

He wears tight jeans and his girlfriend she loves that
'cause she can wear 'em when she's dropping him off
on her way to work, outside the coffee shop.
He trying to mingle, yeah, he's gobbling knobs
trying to score himself a gig or a modelling job.
Then he's wobbling off like he shows no fear

137

feeling real rugged with his overgrown beard.
It's plain now, if he make it as an actor
he gonna be on *Home and Away* then change to an actor
I think his brain's backwards, but I'm a turn it round
this crowbar gonna have him learning how.
He feeling urban now, but it can change quick
have him running back to Summer Bay with his face split.
Blood spill like paint drips and look beautiful
I'm a use it all just to paint me a mural
got kids finger painting, shit gets realer
'cause they gonna grow up to be some Hipster Killers!

Who am I?
I'm a Hipster Killer!

Untitled
LORNA MUNRO

Your genesis
Was baseless

Place less

Australian redneck racists
Get back on your convict slave ships
Go home
We don't need you no more
Lets face it …

I've been dreaming of a land before time
I've been needing a lil' place I can call mine

I've been fading
Sinking into my cemented boots I'm out of line
How do I change it?
Where can I feel weightless?
And fly

Over rated
Cage less
Break even all that you made us …
The balance was there to save us
Are we so complacent to beg for a revolution,
But never wanna make any changes?

Tweaking our views from our mirrors
Checking blind spots
Did you miss the plot?
It was stolen …
What wealth has your mind got?
When your head remains in the gutter

A crime spot

Where their masters
Keep them lines locked
Punching in time sheets
A record of all the jobs
They never got …

That week

I found it hard to speak

Thinking of TJ, David, Elijah, Miss Dhu and Patrick
Still I dream on
Because this life is nothing that I wanna rely on
No shoulder to cry on
But a sista with a voice
That make ya wanna shine on

Call on

The strength of my blood
My ancestors learned to swim
While the rest of the 'evolving' world
Escaped the flood
Give all my time and live in love
My legs refuse to get tired of
Standing ground
So I watch the clouds above

#Justice4Pat
#Justice4Elijah
#Justice4MissDhu
#Justice4TJ

Still no justice for David Gundy

I run …
MELANIE MUNUNGGURR-WILLIAMS

I like to call myself a runner
Cos that's what I do
When life attacks me from all angles like I'm a paper bag in a
    thunderstorm
I run
I run from all my problems, tune out all sounds of day and life
Until the only sound I'm left with is my feet hitting the tarmac, carrying
    me away
My heart thumping deep within the lonely, hollow, cavity of my chest
I run
I do fun-runs and marathons to escape cyclonic turmoil, Run through rivers
    in the hope my scent will get lost in the currents
But like a black tracker, my problems find me
They chase me down the way white authorities chased down brown-skin
    babies,
Hold me captive the way this country holds asylum seekers and taunt me
the way my abuser does, despite me already
leaving the scene of that crime
I run

I run through beautiful boundaries that segregate real from true,
Run into a blur of horizons of sadness and the gravitational pull of a
    woman going mad
Nice girl to bitch, good guy to asshole, the cycle posing the same question
    as, 'What came first?
The chicken or the egg?'
And the answer … no one really knows
But personal perspective tells me the nice girl came before the asshole who
    created the bitch
And now I'm stuck with trying to run from her,
That beat down beauty
Suicidal psycho caught between the western white-man's world
and ancient Aboriginal antiquity

I run

I run to the hills and sing my praises to my inner child cos she reminds
    me of the beauty of a rainbow in the rain,
The excitement of mud between my toes,
The happiness of life's simplicities, she
Is the first pearl in my ocean

I run to the ocean where all my tears from years past have collected,
    knowing that if I blow it a kiss the least it will do is wave back, and if
    I'm lucky

My salty sweat from all that I have run from
Will one day
Bathe me clean

The boys
OMAR MUSA

The boys are turning mad.
The boys are turning circles in the sky.
The boys are swooping down
with bass-heavy hearts & sharps talons,
plucking the eyes of cows & dismembering doves.

   The boys are turning ferocious.

The boys are growing up
     with garlands of nuts, bolts & knucklebones
          around their necks.
Pistons plunge
     in their forearms & jaws,
     petrol churns
          in the chambers of their chests.

They trade dynamite for candles
     & whip words in the cake mix
     – *slut, bitch, whore, lowy, ganga, mutt.*

They confront each other with the tenderness of wild things
     & the brutality of the civilised –

the boys are *turning* on each other.

The boys are turning *on* each other –
     they are getting hard at the thought of carnage,
     drawing lines on the bodies of women,
          like rich man on map,
          like butcher on diagram of beast.

The boys are turning on the fulcrum of history,
     enraged at the thought that things might change
     from the way they have always been.

I know this
    because I have dreamed their raptor dreams.

The boys are turning away.
They are turning into fathers & busdrivers & poets,
    uncles & bosses & boyfriends.
In servos & boardrooms, in courtrooms & pubs,

    The boys are turning into men.

Human
ANISA NANDAULA

I was in grade three.
I sat beside a pale boy with eyes coloured like all the oceans he was yet to cross.
I sneezed.
With shock that electrocuted every assumption swimming through his
    nine-year-old body,
He gasped.
'I didn't know Africans sneezed.'
I laughed.
He laughed too.
It was at that moment he realised I was like him.
Human.

Moe mai rā
NGĀ HINEPŪKŌRERO

Because she was barren she daydreamed about children
And grasping a takawai she composed a lullaby
He wahine, he whenua, e ngaro ai te tangata
She was a music lover
A melodious metaphor she would press to her chest
As the feathers of her korowai fell
They floated
And she changed from being the property of her father
To the property of her husband
He wahine, he ipo, kua ngaro ai ia
She played her role in te ao Māori
Like the men played the pūkāea
Ka moe koutou rā
She was taught to link
The past
The present
And the future
Ki waenga i te korowai
But her whare tangata
Was a meeting house with no manuhiri
O ure tārewa
Her reo was softer than the petals of her skin
It was frail and wilting
Dying for a fire that won't spark in her kōpū
Moe mai rā
Her mind wanders more than her body ever has
Aku tōtara haemata
She's a pūrerehua
And her frayed string was never tied
We hear her song in the confines of our bedrooms
Lulling us to sleep
The taste of metallic
On her tongue
As she sang
A takawai filled with tears

For a child born dead
Leaving a parent with a life sentence
Convicted of murder before another life could be lost
She has jail bars forming in her womb
And she sees her unborn child
In the creases of her tear-stained face

Why do Māori women have so many problems?

Why do you have so much to fucking say?
Do you understand what it's like
To be told you are sacred
Because of a gift you didn't ask for
So your rights are stolen away from you like the babies that you're forced
    to produce
And if your machine is broken
Well then so are you
Do you understand what it means to lose a child
To be cowered over their limp bodies
They're not dying because they want to
We're killing them
They're punching bags with fresh bruises to mark the passage of time
Pockmarking them until their tiny hands no longer shake
And only death would liberate them from this cruelty they never deserved
    to face

Moko
Nia
Hinekawa
Terepo

We'll do anything to keep them safe
If it means you'll stuff cotton wool down our oesophagus
We'll choke until our begging is heard
If you paint our bodies to cover our pain
We'll wash our faces until our mascara runs red
Even if our wombs weren't made to hold children
We will not let the kids that could have been ours

Be murdered in living rooms behind closed curtains

Moe mai rā
Her takawai began to slip through her hands
Moe mai rā
She was losing her grip
Moe mai rā
The takawai stopped breathing
And she crumbled like the earth beneath her feet

You can't be black
STEVEN OLIVER

You can't be black
When the media shows Aborigines they live on communities
And struggle with petrol, poverty and disease
So you can't be black
If you were black you wouldn't have nice clothes on your back
You'd probably wanna try and attack me because of the morality you lack, see?
So you can't be black
See I understand every word that you say, you speak in an educated way
Talk of being Prime Minister one day so, you can't be black
You live in the suburbs, have a nice car, have the tidiest yard by far
Sip on a martini in a trendy bar, go overseas and travel afar
You talk about your law degree, your plan to save humanity, you volunteer with Amnesty
So you can't be black because don't you see that they're the things I want to be
And when I look at you I don't see me though I can't define just what that means but you
Can't be black

20 questions
JESSE OLIVER

People sometimes ask me …

1.   What's it like to be trans?
2.   What's it like to not be able to stand as you are?
3.   As you were?
4.   Him?
5.   Or her?
6.   Which is it?
7.   What's the deal with pronouns?
8.   Why does your voice sound strange?
9.   If you start taking T, can you ever go back again?
10. How the hell does sex work?
11. Do your genitals start to grow?
12. Have you even figured out to which bathroom you're going to go?
13. What day did you realise?
14. What ways did you disguise?
15. Can you even tell me why?
16. Why?
17. Why don't you like your tits?
18. And what sort of bits have you got?

And here I am left standing here like …

19. What?

Still, they look me up and down with a half frown as I drown in their questions
in their quest to find out which labels suit me best.

It's a little from column A and a little from B, you see, the thing about me,
is I could be two or three, four or more of anything at any one time.
Just like I rhyme, and sometimes I don't.

So asking me is not the best. Let's give it a rest, it's tiring.
What we need is some rewiring and hopefully I'm inspiring a new way
without foul play, like maybe spend the day.
Let's hang out. Find out what I'm about without tearing me apart.
I'll tell you where to start, you can reach my brain through my heart.

Because nothing beats the soft touch of trust and knowing you care so
    much
to actually discover me, and my gender details subsequently.
It is a large part of who I am, but I am not just a man.
I'm more than my body, this is just something I own.
Don't ask about testosterone, don't ask me about how I made this my
    home.

Ask if I like coffee.

If you do too, we'll get some and then we'll see where that story ends.
Because if we're honest …

   20.   Don't we only open up to our friends?

You see more on foot
SEAN O'CALLAGHAN

I put my hood up
and it's cold
not deathly or bitter
just cold enough
to keep your cheeks alive and
open your eyes
that bit further
to see the full moon
silver and grey glowing
with clouds that drift
quickly past it
above the auto-repair sign
that hangs on the wire fence
where the barking mutt protects
an oul wrecked house
with a boat in the garden and
some dead cars
on the way to a 7-Eleven
on foot
for a bar of chocolate
with a cup of tea Jodie
always wants in the evening
on the warm sofa
in front of the heater
which is too expensive
when you have no money
but the moon over
the auto-repair shop sign
is free and
the cold air that
springs my cheeks to life
is free
but the fish and chips
I drove down for aren't
so I get the chocolate turn around

notice other things
you can only notice walking
pay
get in my car and
drive right at
the big fat moon that makes the night

Ways to draw blood from feathers
ANGELA PEITA

1. The coming of the rain brought the earthworms to meet
   the surface. Blinded and exposed they remind me of swimming
   naked in the ocean.
   Tattered crows flock to find their breakfast, today will not be
   the day they starve.
   Is rain the continuation of life, or the beginning of death?

2. Wherever you have gone, you have always been flanked by
   birds of prey. Like any enmeshed attachment, I am never sure
   if it is you that seeks them – or they you.
   When we come across a caged eagle amongst the other birds in
   the aviary, you begin to cry.
   With the slipstream of feathers that follows you, you are
   broken by this single one. This bird will never find you. You will
   only see it again if you return to its cage.

3. I come across some birds I recognise and it sparks something
   in me. Peering through crowded cages I conjure bolt cutter
   images, ponder what the penalty is for bird smuggling.
   I wonder if they were caught without their paperwork, snagged
   in bureaucratic netting on their flight to freedom.

4. The storms here are louder and brighter than in our city. I
   measure space with my hands to see if this place is closer to
   sky. Overhead birds circle though thunderclaps fearlessly.
   It's beautiful, and you raise your hands and wait for the lightning.

5. The time I decided to get wings tattooed across my back
   so you could never keep me prisoner again.

Of books and bookcases
KIRI PIAHANA-WONG

My boyfriend says that
the one new thing he's
learnt about me since
we moved in together
is that I leave my
books lying around
all over the house.

It's true. I like to
be surrounded by
books, all their
different colours and
sizes, a wall of
words.

I tell him that the one
thing I've learnt about
him is that for a
cabinet-maker, he
doesn't own much
furniture.

I remind him of how
he won my heart by
promising to build me
bookcases for *all* my
books. He just
smiles, arranging the
books in towering
piles against the
wall.

Memo
∏.O.

a Bomb threat
will inevitably come as a shock.
If you receive one [Don't let on!]
Keep the caller talking;
Ask him [or
her!] when the bomb will explode; Where it is;
What it looks like;
And what will c a u s e it to explode;
Ask the caller
their name; And how old they are;
Take particular notice
of their accent: Israeli-German, Spanish-Russian;*
And to their tone: Angry. Drunk.
Calm. Excited; If you happen to know
who they are . don't . let . on
Don't blurt-out: 'Hey! That you? Bob!'
… jus' keep 'em talking; Listen to
background noise: a train whistle could be a vital clue!
When the caller
has finished: DON'T HANG UP!
Keep calm; And write in clear legible
script: WE'RE GOING TO BE BOMBED!!!!!!!!!!!!
And then hand it to
your Supervisor [: He'll know
what to do]; If the ORDER to evacuate, is not given
open all the doors and windows [to lessen
the effect on property damage] and go back
to your desk, and keep
working.

---

* substitute latest tyrants

156

Te Rarangatira
TE KAHU ROLLESTON

Te Puna
Springs to mind when I reminisce on the initial gathering of all of us.
Together, at Paparoa, we were safe and secure within the Mauri of the Moana.
Natives! Feeding off the light and rising to the skies like the Kauri and Tōtara.

Together, we created moments.
Moments like . . .
When you step into the pōwhiri
And your ope begins to kōkiri.
Through the air and the earth,
The tupuna of your iwi
Converse
And you reply with vibrations through your kōiwi.

We created moments.
That added to the muka ka apapa on which this Te Raranga tira korowai has been woven.

We were interwoven by the force of the the four winds. Ngā hau e whā.
A generation of natives with aspirations of going far.
Some peaceful warriors, others of Tūmatauenga.

Regardless.
Together as one we created moments.

Moments like … with these giants by my side.
Afraid of heights we walked the sky.

Skating on tree branches.
Feet planted 20 feet above the ground.
We moved through the clouds.
We moved in leaps and bounds.

In an instant, lifetime friendships were found.
Bonds were bound.
As we created moments.

Moments like on Te Tairāwhiti together as one, we shared the air.
We breathed the air and listened to whispers of our ancestors actions that echoed stories through our ears.

We were guided along this journey. By some of its kaitiaki.
We were safe. Escaped away from the technological trap and life-sized hīnaki.

We created moments in a place before this.
To me was only a myth.

A place where the free reign of warua exists.
A place that just is.

Preserved in the kōrero and waiata of my tīpuna. Mai I Ngā Kurī ā Whārei.

I've always known where that is.
Now I can finally say I've journeyed to where Tihirau lives.
A place overshadowing Puketapu at Te Taunga Waka. The boundary of Mataatua's grips.
And we breathed its air.

We breathed the air, and shared the breath of our ancestors, salted by the ocean ever so slightly.
As we observed Tirairaka dance in the light breeze.
We received stories of great voyages to and from Hāwaiki.

We watched Tāwhiri's breeze
blow through Tāne's trees.

We watched Tangaroa gently greet Papa along the beach below.
In a frame preserved in the picturesque of centuries ago.

As we stood atop the maunga, listening to thousand year old history of waka,
we attempted to buffer, the esoteric barrier for but a minute with haka.

As we scattered amongst the hills' peaks
We listened and allowed ourselves to hear the hill's peak.
And tell us stories only birds mountains and hills speak.

From atop this maunga.
Hungry, in search of a new adventures we voyaged to Heretaunga.

Where we felt,
As if he cast us himself.
To uplift a motu. At least partly.
We pierced through Tangaroas sea on Te Matau a Maui
Blinded but guided right and left, left and right, matau and mauī.

Basically what I'm here to ask. Is have you felt secure?
I don't mean seatbelt secure.
I mean safe to be yourself,
Within yourself, secure.
Because I have.

Sean, Shawn, Shorn, Shaun: these I have known
TESSA ROSE

(Sean) Quirk Street, Manly Vale,
the sheen of premium unleaded, so sexy,
slick over your lips and chin. You breathe fire,
and spin a stick of flame in lazy arcs around the
backyard. It's 1998, so this is still cool.
I am impressed, later,
when you light a Stuyvesant,
petrol clinging still to your beard.
You will marry a girl named Camille.

(Shawn) When, across the tops
of slender arms,
my longing grows, pale
and downy, when it covers
my face and thighs,
you are the only man
I know to tell me
my body frightens you.

(Shorn) Kathmandu, someplace lonely
you're on the hunt for the oracle,
the miracle, the mystery you've heard so
much about, from lithe, henna-bellied
women from your kundalini yoga class.

You are not high or lithe enough to find it,
so you take to your hair with a pair of shitty scissors,
in front of the mirror in the hotel bathroom.
It's like that one scrape when
the peddler sold Anne Shirley the hair dye
and it all went wrong.
She had to shear off the whole fucking lot of it.

(Shaun) And on the first day
Shaun said

I think those pills, those
pink ones I sold you? I think
there's acid in them.
Sorry.
And on the second day
I said
Oh yeah?

Impermanent
CANDY ROYALLE

Those whispers that were present
and fell like feathers onto the bed
we should never have laid in together
wept their own secrets onto sheets
of minimum thread

Restricted totally by the binds we
roped round the sounds our mouths made
to halt longings not meant to be uttered
we held back just enough
so those lives we couldn't have lived forever

didn't intrude on this
impermanent heaven of never
Had you bothered asking for honesty
I would have answered honestly:
truth is not my forte

so should you lay with me
know when you submit
it is to small offerings
the tumult of bodies
in the tangle of sheets

those constant reminders to breathe
are all you're going to get
whatever is hidden
remains so for a reason
it's not for either of us to dig

know we can never trade
this piece of small for something big

Old guys

MAX RYAN

get to the club every evening early
with wives called Betty, Flo or Shirley

order the mixed grill and chips with lots of gravy
look loud if they're not in something grey or beigey

always wear their trousers way too high
will wave if they've seen you once or twice

sometimes have a piece of one ear missing
let the news about the operation just slip in

always miss a loop on their belt band
eat spaghetti that comes in a tin can

always look sad when they're on their own
get there too late to catch the phone

read the death notices like they read the weather
see they're not there and somehow feel better

old guys are everywhere, with their toast and tea
old guys are starting to look like me

How to live in a world that is burning
OMAR SAKR

1. There are many kinds of vision

2. The nurse said getting glasses has been on her
to-do list since 2008   It's a long list
but also, the world is burning
& what is the point of seeing all the colours
fire can become   if it all turns to ash

3. I haven't figured out how to live
                    in an unburned world & so
I hesitate to put out the flames

4. The nurse can't see distances
It is the curse of our lazy, entitled generation
she laughs. This is her second shift of the day
& it is getting hard to see how not to laugh

5. The older patient beside me can only see distances
Between the two   I hover in the void

6. I am constantly hard here

& not just because I suspect the gay couple
have been sucking each other off in the showers
a fluid exchange of themselves

7. I am bled every day
    & watching the red river
snake out   reminds my body
    it is alive & dying

8. How can such a thin tube contain all the countries
        in my skin   so many spewing mountains

9. The world be burning &
          drowning at the same time
a tumult of land & sea welcomed
only by the winged &
          even they can falter on a hot wind

10. Anything seen
    through watery flames
    wavers

11. The ultimate goal of hardness
is to soften   as the ultimate goal
of fire   is to change   no matter the cost
everything burns

12. This is the part where I am meant
to offer you grace,   dear Phoenix I am
meant to say: rise

InshaAllah
SARA SALEH

In my language, inshaAllah means: forever
In my language, inshaAllah means: love, forever

It means no, *everything* is no.

It means, whenever something stops working, you'll fix it, inshaAllah …
    eventually.
Or it means, you'll call your brother's wife's uncle's cousin to fix it instead.

InshaAllah means '*ahla w sahla*' – welcome, whenever you come.
It will when He wills, mama and baba will work it out.
And if they don't, inshaAllah means you are their battleground,
middle-ground, peacemaker. But nothing about this world
is peaceful and fears are often shaped like
humans.

InshaAllah means I can't have you out late, girl,
the playgrounds came dressed as checkpoints,
and boys with guns are the same everywhere.

InshaAllah means I will take care of you. I wear stains in my palms
where my mother's hand or candy should be.

It means we are safe, don't worry, the bombs are in Burj and Sabra and
    Damascus …
InshaAllah means, we are used to it.

InshaAllah means you'll find a job, even
when they come to take it. It is not their
fault, they are from that stillborn country.

InshaAllah means we do what we can, inshaAllah means I know
you're worried, this world is a burning building.

InshaAllah means there are many worlds. Maybe in one, you are not dead.

It means the men might not return home from war, there is always war.

It means I make prayer, I make
places holy. And my holy place
is you.

InshaAllah is my greeting to the divine
– time, love, family, fear, death, how I try to know
the unknowns … the next moment knows what the one before never even
    suspected.

InshaAllah is my inheritance, a nostalgia for my long
lost, for a place that no longer exists. InshaAllah is the answer
when there are still questions but no answers to give.

It means the many homes – and the
none.

It means someone play Abdel Halim
She might be a western girl, but her *mawal*, her melody is eastern.
She is all 'ahhhhs' and 'ouffsssss'.

InshaAllah means their hate will break even that
which does not bend. Even hate. Even you.

It means so much of this year is flammable. Like shopping lists, like
love letters, like birth certificates.

InshaAllah means I am sorry they named you biological clock. Our bodies
    are trending.

InshaAllah means one day I will understand why I have my
father's accent, and that poems do not
solve things, but I'll keep writing
anyway.

It means maybe one day, I'll tell our child, You come from
a long line of words,
of song, of poetry.

InshaAllah means goodbye, dear.

InshaAllah what I mean to say is, I want your
music, I mean I want your midnights, I want your
mistakes ... Most of all ... I want your
InshaAllahs

No security blues
BEN SALTER

I cannot complain
I must not complain
I've got some problems, sure
But they are not real problems

And Will can't get the sand out of his shoes

I lie here and listen
With the no security blues

I've got more than most, more
'more than most' than 'less than some'
And what is this one per cent that you speak of?
Cause I cannot complain
I don't have real problems
There's a storm out there that scares the great aunts
And great uncles
There's a flare-up in some far-off land
That threatens to get out of hand
As I lie in at ten a.m.
Trying to decide just
Where I stand

And I've got nothing much to lose

No security blues

Is it a win/win?
Or will I lose lose lose?
I must not think
Just do
No security blues

I will read the paper
With my tea and my toast

Left to my devices
Well I'm doing better than most

And these are not real problems

Well my eyes are bad and my teeth are weak
But this is what I choose:

I have no marketing blues
I have no sand in my shoes
I have no pending law suits
I have ninety-nine problems
But they are not real problems

I have no blues

I've never had the blues

I have no security blues

Well the bank just called again
Seems I have everything to lose
But I have no real problems
Just some credit card issues
And the no security blues

The Catholic-Mobile
RAY SHIPLEY

I learnt to drive stick shift in a van of questionable road-worthiness
Borrowed from Mother Mary (full of grace)
Who knew, though we didn't ask her
And who saw, although she was not there, really –
Her statue stood on the dash
Hands praying, paint chipping, rosary beads hitting her or me in the face when I stalled
Naturally, we baptised the van *The Catholic-Mobile.*

Jesus was in the front seat in the body of a smoking, cursing ex-Catholic who didn't believe in deodorant
God was in the back seat who, having not found a working seatbelt, had my headrest in a death grip
The Holy Spirit was there too –
    she was the lights of Sumner reflected on the water,
      the 'danger – nature was greater than this diff' sign that we ignored,
      she was the sound of late night birds in trees unseen
She was of course in the van too –
    she was the smell of old incense and muddy football boots,
    each shudder and kick of the engine,
    each sharp intake of God's breath,
    each *Holy shit* Jesus uttered,
    she was the redness of my knuckles

173

I learnt to drive stick shift up a cracked hill and down the other side, shouting *Save us* as we crunched gravel

Accelerated accidentally and by some miracle, parked perfectly

We tumbled out of the van, firm atheists again

Announcing that we were fools and I was better off driving an automatic.

She remained.

In the sand between our toes and the echoes of laughter on the cliffs, she remained.

She remained in the hollow shells of crabs

And in the sound and the knowledge of the waves crashing long before we arrive and long after we leave she remained

And she remained although we exhaled and exclaimed wasn't it so beautiful to have this

And not have to believe in sea monsters or fairies at the bottom of the ocean or the bottom of the garden as well

And so we praised great writers and dreamers and non-believers

And she sighed through the trees and

She remained anyway.

W.O.W.
STEVE SMART

Hi, it's me, your friend
you invited me round
now I'm sitting on the couch
while you play computer games

if you'd invited anyone else
I'd have someone to talk to at least
you said we were going out
you just had to finish a level
there was a crazy thing that
you wanted to show me
totally fucked up
sick man

It was pretty cool, but
that was an hour and a half ago
you're on your 5th level
and your 6th bong

you've stopped
speaking

you're very
intense

there are
monsters
to be killed

WOW!
World of Warcraft

I'd ask for a turn
but it's not really that sort of game
and we both know I'm crap

I'd wreck your progress
you'd have to go back to the last save
we'd never get out of here

we may still
never get out of here

I've read the back of the box blurb four times
scanned the TV guide twice, thrice
there's still nothing good on
I could watch a video
but I want to get off this couch
out of this room, I want to go out

you have no booze!

the pub will shut soon
I fear we'll be here all night
I fear neither of us will ever get laid again

you can't understand
why chicks don't dig video games
you don't understand 'chicks'
and their weird need for 'conversation'

you don't realise that some of your friends
alsohaveaweirdneedforconversation

I start to hum
(*mm mmm mmm mmmmm mm*)
you tell me to shut up
I'm breaking your concentration
I'm being annoying

I break a chair over your head
(in my imagination)
((you don't notice))

I should leave
I don't want to go out by myself
I think there's a party on
I can't remember where

I stand up
it's 2 a.m.
I say I'm going
you grunt
Catch you later

I walk outside
the night air is cool
I walk down the street
waiting for the monsters to appear
but they're all busy
inside your head

I consider going out
but I've lost the will
I go home alone, play
Command and Conquer 'til dawn

postiche

AMANDA STEWART

nnnnnnnnnnow

now
now
now that distance is solved
difference resolved
now that you can
now that it isn't

post-post prereformation
empires crumble reform the next location

as self the mean of generalisation in the individual's back pocket
a reflexive net across difference a finite law within
everything's relative in the doctrine of commodities
post-renaissreconnaissance body transcending in a stockmart of

realiterity inducing abstractionscheap banality deducing reduction

for your convenience

high above on a Plato of strategy

      an internet sky channels into a privatised black hole

      a host of bob's boys r r rise

from the ashes of socialism

sacrificial lam whit t l e d from the consensus of mates

born-again-bureaus meet next-to-be-business-boomers

murd ocked in a tabloid of now is a pay for the right to

say, 'I still call Austr a i d i n g the integrated verticals of

capitalised fate

                    outta here!

Tinā (Mother)
GRACE TAYLOR

hissing glass laughs

slap her face

as the gods throw stones at her empty bucket

her arms house voices

full fat as horses veins

bulging rock solid

she presses her feet

deep into the bloody grass

soaking up the crosses of fallen men

a storm of a woman

->

my mother married her malu alone

I was too afraid to witness

tap   tap

blood   ink

when I returned home

she lay healing

bloody pillows soaking up the tufuga work

we take her to dip

freshly carved into the mouth of Maraetai

soaking salts to cuts

returning blood back to the vasa

I should have been the vasa

<-

they say ancestors dance on her skin

when she siva Samoa

they say she moves the old way

makes Tagaloa beg for more

the vasa reminiscc

and seeds absorb

when she siva Samoa

she dances on ancestors skin

An early survey of principles

SANDRA THIBODEAUX

During the Live Cattle Trade crisis, three Indonesian teenagers appeared in an
Australian court, arguing against their imprisonment in an adult jail. They had worked
on an asylum seeker boat.

Two unreliable lovers
cancel each other out.

Stunning hair
eclipses a plain face.

Sometimes, a moth
will do everything to die.

*

An Aussie flag on the pecs
= a Redneck above.

1 Australian steer
> 3 Indonesian teens.

An Andrew Bolt minus an Andrew Bolt
can only be a good thing.

*

There are two sides to a turtle
but no argument for a 4WD on her tracks.

Running feet
leave their arguments in the sand.

A crocodile leaves an 's'
and the feeling's mutual.

*

Frogs resist
offers of rescue.

A snake has nowhere better to go
than your bed.

The last cane toad
wasn't.

*

The distance to an extraordinary lover
is > 1,000 kilometres.

The number of times he texts
is < encouraging.

A replacement in your bed
is less than, or equal to, sweet notes on a horn?

*

Distant lovers
come close in the archives.

An athlete's heart
jumps a forgettable face.

A moth + an open door
= a new way to dance

Assimilation
TAYI TIBBLE

they consider
themselves to be
a modern couple

they take turns

giving
and receiving
oral

they split the bills
evenly and they share
the chores but

when he brings in
the washing
he leaves the pegs
all over the ground

he doesn't bother to
pick them up
and put them back
into the basket

and she considers this to be
culturally insensitive

and as progressive
as they are
she can't help

but think about
potatoes and muskets
disease-ridden blankets
surveyors and preachers

and how many Māori girls
ended up on their knees
in order to erect
this modern nation

she sighs
and rolls her eyes
like a tiny haka

as she pulls the last
remaining peg embedded
in the mud with the last
of her mana

she could either lick them clean
with the sponge of her tongue

or

plunge them back into the earth's
dark wet cunt. Let her husband pick them up.

Moonface and me
MERLYNN TONG

[Hello everybody!! How are you? Good? Good. Nice to meet you! So many white people. So nice! Very nice. Anyway, my name is Millie. M-I-L-L-I-E. It's a very cool name okay. I tell you in Singapore right, not many people have this name. It's very special. Like me. I tell you, my world is very special! Like right now, right now. All my favourite things are here.]

There is a big tree. But the tree trunk is made out of Cordon Bleu bottle – my favourite. Have you drunk it before? It's so good. And the branches are all white, smooth Virginia Slims cigarettes and the leaves, the leaves are all transparent. Let me taste. It's tears. But but look at the sky! It's a moon! No! It's 17 moons! So white, so beautiful. I like this one. Let me touch it. OOH! You know what it reminds me of? My John. Ya John is not a very special name. But he is a very nice man. Okay, remember that John is a very nice man. And touching this moon, reminds me of him because when I touch his face, it's like touching the moon. It is rough and then smooth, it juts out and then it dip dips and dips in. Sometimes he lets me press the pus out of his face too. Squeeze. Mmmm. But his moon face is so beautiful when I run my hands on the smooth, rough, hard, soft, dry, prickly, tender, soft bits. I love staring at this moon face when he sleeps. And I love touching his face. He's a quiet man this John so in order to unravel, reveal, expose and tear apart his walls to see his stories, you have to touch his moon face. This dip underneath his chin whispers the story of the time when he was training in East Timor and a knife pushed through his skin. See these hollow caves on his right cheek? They rage about the teenage years when John was always made fun of for being smart and wearing spectacles that went across half his face. Oh this part. The smoothness of the skin right above his eye sings songs about his love for my two children. And this bulge, this bulge right beside his nose exposes his secret desire to have children of his own.

One moon 2 moons 3 moons, 4, 5, 6, 7, 8, 9, 10, 11, 12, 13, 14, 15, 16, 17. 17 moons. 17 moon faces. 17 Johns. I want to put them all in my mouth so I can hold not 1, not 2 but 17 mini Johns in my belly. Maybe if I just start myself and he joins in later …

MILLIE pleasures herself. MILLIE becomes JOHN.

[Hello everyone, my name is John. So I'm here to tell you a story. You know I don't have many stories. Just one. It's a love story. I know I don't look like the kind of guy who has love stories. But I have one. One love story. Like so many love stories, mine starts in the ...]

Wartime East Timor 1999! Everywhere around me it's BOOM BOOM BOOM BOOM BOOM BOOM. And I stand here behind my bush. I hold my hard cold gun in my hand. But it's not loaded. Still I hold it, pose it like it can be used for something. I can see nothing around me but I can hear them. I can hear them. They're close. I tell myself, 'Be a man! Be a man! I've got my training I got this.' But it haunts my head that my gun is not loaded. I am with the UN and my gun is not loaded. All I have to protect me is this bush. This little bush barely bigger than my body. No one else with us, Bush. So I sing I sing to her, my little bush. 'Brown leaves hold my head in place, little stems please hide my face, bugs tell them I need some grace. Brown leaves hold my head in place, little stems please hide my face, bugs tell them I need some grace.' Then suddenly it becomes silent. Too silent. I hold on to my impotent gun and the bush starts to shake and brown brown appears. I beg myself not to shit again. And then from under the bush more brown appears. Brown brown brown skin. It is a woman. Big round fish ball eyes. It is my future wife.

He dances with his wife and chants 'BOOM BOOM BOOM' repeatedly.

One day I had one computer, internet connection and four minutes. Darling, just give me some time, I just need to break things off with Millie.

JOHN becomes MILLIE.

My big strong police officer sent my daughter an email. Is that what you call it? EMAIL? Stupid name. My daughter was so excited she ran to me and said, 'Mummy, Mummy, Uncle John wrote you an email!' I did not know what that was but I was excited too. And we ran back to the computer. I could not see the words. I pretended it was because I had a headache but really I was getting old. I can't see clearly anymore. So I said, 'You read to me girl'. 'You read to me girl' I said that. And her young sweet lips poured out those disgusting mothball-smelling words. Rotten fish. Garbage words. I can't remember what it was exactly but I remembered feeling barren. But

187

I was not. I may be old and fat but my womb is still healthy, strong and hungry. But I cannot. I cannot have any more children. My daughter and my son are enough. Strange enough. I don't know what I'm doing with them. I don't want to ruin more lives. If only I could do it. Have a child with him.

I stand at my full-length mirror and look at myself. I am like a pear, a soggy rotten pear. I hold the meat off my belly, it feels like dough, ready, with potential to become something something, waiting, but nothing happens. My face once so beautiful now of a woman I haven't got to know. Did not take the time to get to know. But why would I? She crept in and took over my body. I noticed her invasion at one point. And I cycled and swam to keep her away. But she kept coming back.

John is a very nice man. So I did what I had to. I went to my tree. I wiped away the leaves. I smoked away the branches. I ate all 17 Moons. Moonface. John. Darling boys. Sayang. Quickly now, quickly. Before I lose courage like the last time. And now I drink the whole trunk.

Student day

SABA VASEFI

Next to crumpled green flyers
By the debris piled behind the half-built house
Does anyone know of the girl tripped in Alexandra Street
And the odd shoe
Left behind far away from my feet?
Does anyone know of the claws pulled my hand
And the yelling
That stayed behind in my mind and hastened my visa to run?
I was lobbed over to this edge of the globe
Breathing comes hard again
Though there's no tear gas at work
Nor even a napkin drenched in vinegar
Held by the hand of a friend to my mouth
I am sitting like a piece of mud stuck to the sole
Does anyone know of my black shoe
Whose pair is sitting in grief of the other
Waiting on the shelf of my room?

شانزده آذر

صبا واصفی

کنار کاغذ مچاله های سبز
پشت خاک تپه ی آن خانه ی نیمه ساز
کسی می داند آیا
از سکندری خورده دختری
در خیابان اسکندری
و لنگه کفشی
بی وصل و دور افتاده از پاهام؟
از دست سگ مستی که دستم را کشید
و عربده ای
که در ذهن من جا مانده ویزای فرارم فوری کرد
کسی می داند اینک چیزی؟
پرتاب شدم به انتهای جهان
نفسم تنگ است باز
گاز اشک آوری در کار نیست
دستمالی سرکه ای حتی
دستی که با دهانم رفیق باشد هم
مثل گِل نشسته ام
بر کفِ کفش
کسی سراغ ندارد آیا
از لنگ کفش سیاهم
که لنگه اش
در سوگ لنگه ی دیگر
روی رف اتاقم
نشسته منتظر؟

190

When pencils sing excuses
SAM WAGAN WATSON

A MESSAGE TO MY PUBLISHER: I'm sorry you haven't seen or heard from me; I've been lost in a good poem, I've been travelling with a dictionary of freaks, I've been teaching pencils to sing … A MESSAGE TO MY PUBLISHER: A message in a bottle, dictated from bottles, trying to muse a Tom Waits three-day growth and growl *and I'd rather have a bottle in front of me than a frontal lobotomy … Ahhhh!* I'm sorry I haven't called, I'm sorry I didn't write you a note, I'm sorry I didn't write you that manuscript that's five years in the making and I've got enough excuses to fill five manuscripts … I've been scribbling excuses just like poems just like excuses just like rectums and everyone has a rectum, has excuses, has poems coming out of their rectums, and every rectum is a critic! The dog ate my manuscript. My granny died … again. *Ahhhh!* A MESSAGE TO MY PUBLISHER: I've been lost in a good poem, I've been travelling with a dictionary of freaks, I've been teaching pencils to sing, I've been filing excuses in bottles, bottles been filling me with messages, *PLEASE, CALL YOUR PUBLISHER* … 'Cause I need to find myself from inside that good poem. I need to stop showcasing a dictionary of freaks. And I need to switch off the muse, inside the sweet voices of pencils …

Give nothing
TAIKA WAITITI & EMILY BEAUTRAIS

As New Zealander of the Year,
I'm calling on every one of my fellow Kiwis
to help support a very important cause.

Racism

needs your help to survive.

You may not be in a position to give much to racism,
but whatever you feel comfortable giving
will make a huge difference.

You don't have to be a full-on racist,
just being a tiny bit racist is enough.

A smile, a cheeky giggle, even a simple nod in agreement,
it all adds up,
and it gives others the message that it's okay.

FAQaRs
Frequently Asked Questions about Racism

I'm not a real racist. Can I still help?
Of course!
Even if you don't come from a racist background, that's okay.
Being a bit racist is super easy.

How do I spread the word?
You don't actually have to talk people into it,
just be a bit racist, and they'll feel the social pressure to follow along.

My mum says being a bit racist is bad.
Shut up Mum!

What's in it for me?
Ah, nothing. There is no benefit whatsoever to being racist. But ask yourself, what if everyone stopped giving to racism?
What kind of future would that be for our children?

If I only give a little bit, will it even make a difference?
Not to you, no.
But to the people receiving the racism,
they'll be getting hundreds of small bits every day,
so it will add up. It will be noticed.

How do I show my support?
You might not want to wear a T-shirt that says how much of a racist you are.
'No thanks, I'm racist on the inside.'
But you can laugh at racist comments; it does the same thing.
'Ha!'

Remember, the only thing that can keep racism alive
and help it grow,
is feeding it. Nurturing it.
And that's where you come in.

Will you help it flourish?

What will you give to racism?

doctor proctor

ANIA WALWICZ

congratulations for being a doctor doctor congratulations for being a doctor
doctor doctor seuss who hello doctor hello doctor doctor proctor doctor
proctor doctor clover turn me over I don't like the way you are speaking to
me I won't speak to you like this anymore no I won't speak to you like this
anymore how are you ania tired? I'm tired you don't say knackered you don't
say knackered do you do you knackered knackered knackered you don't say
now just trying to be funny don't tell anybody I won't speak to you like this
anymore no good I won't speak to you like this anymore no hello doctor
hello doctor proctor doctor clover roll me over what d'you think you have
done think about what you had done just think about it use your head now
use your head use your head you think you know everything you think you
know everything don't you now miss doctor I like your socks what do you
think that you had done look at it my dog can write better than that you
must ring and ask her to supervise you after all we had done for you after all
we had done congratulations for being a doctor hello doctor doctor proctor
doctor clover roll me over you don't say knackered you congratulations
for being a doctor hello doctor doctor clover turn me over doctor proctor
I won't speak to you like this anymore no I won't speak to you like this
anymore I don't like the way you speak to me I won't speak to you like
this anymore you can use your feminine charm this is excellent excellent
excellent in red pencil on my drawing you never laugh at my jokes why not
look at my little finger now why don't you laugh they thought you were so
clever they thought you were so clever you think that you know everything
why don't you laugh why don't you come I like to tweak you hat I'm sorry
I can't resist this I can't my dog can write better than this what will you get
out of this if you complain what will get out of this if you tell somebody
about this the police will laugh ha ha ha ha I won't speak to you like this
anymore sticks and stones will break my bones this old man he played
drum he played knick knack on my tum knick knack paddywack give a dog
a bone this old man came marching home I won't speak to me anymore
like this I won't speak to you like this anymore hello doctor you have to
knock you can't come in like this you have to knock take you hat off take
your head off d'you ever chit chat? you think you know everything d'you
ever chit chat you should speak about general things and let people come

in you think too much hello doctor who is doctor this is your medal you think too much now just let it go and what will you get out of this if you tell somebody I write that mister wright is a pig I dream that I cut somebody I am cut up don't tell anybody now let it go now there's no point and what's the point you better think what you do think about what you had done was it me professor idiot? did you do that drawing now? was it me tell me did you do this to me? who did this? was it me? did I write this? was it me? who does this to me? who says this? not me I won't talk to you like this anymore congratulations for being a doctor who is doctor doctor proctor doctor clover turn me over was it funny you never laugh at my jokes d'you from your work you can see that you had little experience of life no point in talking about it to anybody it was just humour attempt congratulations for being a doctor doctor proctor doctor clover turn me over I don't like the way you speak to me no I won't speak to you like this anymore how are you ania? tired I am tired you never say knackered you never say knackered knackered knackered this old man he played drum he played knick knack on my tum say knick knack paddywack give a dog a bone this old man came to my home I dream that I cut something I am cut up about this I am cut don't talk about this and don't tell anybody about this they will laugh at my jokes now ha ha ha ha ha dee ha egghead don't believe everything you read congratulations for being a doctor hello doctor doctor proctor doctor clover turn me over sticks and stones will break my bones but words will always hurt me don't be so serious you're too serious d'you think I'm funny? you never laugh at my jokes look at my little finger is it funny what's funny

On all the things I am still learning to name
wāni

1. My name is wāni and on a good day, that's enough
2. I watch full episodes of entire shows in entire seasons all in one day, and I am not ashamed
3. My favourite anime is *One Piece*. There's something about Luffy's constant tenacity that just seems to always get me
4. I have a feeling that even twenty years from now when we finally reach the end of the grand line we still won't know why his dad left him
5. I enjoy long walks to the donut store
6. I am not above petty, I will literally troll white supremacist pages just to like the comments from the black folk roasting the hell out of them
7. That drake and meek mill beef was a real highlight for me
8. I watched a truck slam into a woman once, and nobody said anything. I learnt that day that I'd already internalised so much misogyny it had consumed me, I stood and watched as she attempted to drag herself back onto her feet. She was the first black woman I'd ever seen outside of my own family, and I walked away
9. I keep my mother's words etched on the left side of my left chest pocket for they are the only metaphysical force I've ever known tangible enough to trust
10. I've had far too many people say they want to get to know me like the inside of these hands, only to spend that time searching for reflections of themselves within my body
11. Despite my best efforts I am still learning to love that body
12. Who mourns for little boys who never learnt to say stop
13. Who mourns those little boys that turned to men that won't stop
14. How do I forgive myself for all the things that I tried but couldn't stop
15. Despite my best efforts I am still only a shadow of a guilty conscious fighting between a rock and survivor's guilt
16. I stared down the end of a barrel once, and of all the reasons I could name as to why I am even still standing here, none are because of me
17. I still can't really tell you why that last one was true, but what I do know is I put two bullets in just in case that first one never got through to you

1. There is nothing magic about being surrounded by people who still make you feel lonely
2. I think depression is a strange word, so I prefer work-in-progress
3. I am still a work-in-progress and I am finally okay with that
4. My name is wāni, and on my best days that's enough

This is how we burn the endless woman (an excerpt)
JAHRA 'RAGER' WASASALA

The god has eaten the woman.

I am drunk on gasoline   [strike a match against my teeth]
I have set myself on fire in the middle of your city
No one comes for me.
No one comes. For me.
They just congregate
Warm their hands. Singing stigmata.
[always singing
        without a voice
        within a body
        full of open mouths
        unable to hold
anyone else's language.]

Teethe on a single-tongued translation of labour:
'Daughter' (single-tongue) holding
as the flesh for the skeletal
'retribution' (double-tongue).

The god has eaten the woman.

I have exhausted my possessor   [whoever she is].
She is tired of me   [if she is tired of me, then what is left?].

I am violent! and everyone applauds.
I am soft! and no one believes me.
I walk into your home! naked and joyful.
You take turns naming my body.
I create myth! and everyone sings for me.
I kill the myth! and everyone cries for her.

The god has eaten the woman.

Glory be to the god of consumption.
Glory be to the woman who climbs back up into the mouth.
Glory be to the way this jaw dislocates itself. Make room for mercy.
Glory be to the beauty in my abandonment.
Glory be to the way I have loved so hard
that it has caused old worlds to die
and new worlds to be named
after me.

War
TEILA WATSON (AKA ANCESTRESS)

War the enemy of peace

A rich man's fight

Being fought by the poor

On distant streets

But not so distant shores

Felt the force of First Fleets

The pox was not so small

My peoples decrease

Defending us and our law

Against the dehumanising beast

And where now is our monument,

Recognition of this feat

Our dues

Your people may have died for this

Country

But know that my people did too

And still do

War unannounced

Still not put in the history

Rape and murder on many accounts

The truth of our masses still a

Mystery

Feeling the affects in misdirection

This infection purely clear

You might be fighting wars on other

Shores

But still there's war carried out here

The Australian army troops sent in

Again

But no not to fight and not to defend

Not to fix up but just to condemn

While the rest of white society

Continues to commend

Coz having a fair go

Means having fair skin, white brains

And white friends

The great Australian division

No day of recognition

No land for us to live in

To carry out our own traditions

So can you stand the likes of war?

Can you love, can you adore

A war against culture equality and

Peace?

A human rights law

Is out of play and incomplete

So there's a human rights WAR

Being fought on Aussie streets

War
Yes
The enemy of peace

Tracks
UNCLE HERB WHARTON

Tracks upon the ground
tracks upon the sky
out upon the ocean
you sometimes see the tracks
of ships
since dawning of the Dreamtime
greatest bushmen in the world
did not follow road or maps
always they looked down
to read and follow tracks
no history books did they read
land told all to people
history it was written on the land
the reading told in track.

As Dreamtime began rainbow snake
slide round and round
across the land it slid
it flicked its tail rocks piled up
hollows where it rested
waters where it sleeps
legends from the Dreamtime
the story told in track
embedded in the rocks
tracks a million years old
men of science now read
a message in these tracks

A bushman's life I've led
always following track
a cold clear wintry morning
tracking straying horses down
pausing for a moment
looking upwards to the sky
thirty thousand feet above my head

a clear white vapour trail
jet liner making tracks
across the sky.

That night from comfort of my swag
I track satellite from horizon to horizon
men of science now leave
their tracks up in the sky
even the moon man has
left his track
outward into space among the planets
space probes travel
tracked upon a screen
still secrets from the
Dreamtime and hopes of
future races still
lie in mother earth
Australia's Dreamtime history
not written in a book
upon the earth its written
the story told in track.

You probably think this poem is about you (and it probably is)
SEAN M. WHELAN

Your mother told me that on the night you were born
a fully loaded semitrailer crashed through your front fence
and rolled over spilling hundreds of fresh ripe bananas across your lawn.
I said to her, *What do you think that meant?*
She said, *Two ambulance officers down with broken limbs while trying to
sprint through*
a minefield of comic relief to aid in your premature birth.

Your father told me that as a teenager
you chewed gum like a horse on amphetamines
dressed like a blind aerobics instructor
and told anyone who would listen
that bananas were Satan's handguns.
He also told me that every night you didn't stay at home
He'd stand on the back porch and chain-smoke
petrified that his daughter wasn't coming home anymore.
And one night you didn't …

Your grandmother told me
you used to compare the wrinkles on her hands
to maps of mythical lands.
And every time you'd visit her you would make up a different country for
each hand.
And sometimes the countries of her hands were at war
and you'd flail your grandmother's hands about in the air
until she'd shout for her medication!
But she didn't mind
because your grandmother told me
you knew about the significance of being old
because you had been old before.

The local Catholic priest told me
you stormed into his church one day
and demanded to know
Who put this fire into us?

Which god was responsible?
Was it yours?
He was too afraid to admit that it was his
so he sent you down the road to
to the synagogue and the mosque instead.

Your drug dealer told me
that he had to explain to you that he only sells *illegal* drugs
and that chocolate was pretty much available anywhere.

Your ex-lover told me you used to shout out the names
of each of the four Teenage Mutant Ninja Turtles
while you were having sex
and have no memory of it afterwards.

Your ex-lesbian lover told me
that you used to shout out the names of The Twelve Apostles
while having sex with her
because sex with a woman took longer.

Your housemates told me that one day a week
you took a vow of silence and only communicated
to the rest of the house through interpretive dance.
They told me that compiling a shopping list on that day
was an exhausting ordeal.

Your best friend told me
that you told me you loved me once.
I said, *Why don't I remember that?*
She said, because you told me you loved me
through interpretive dance.
I thought you were choking
and tried to perform the Heimlich manoeuvre on you.

And you told me
that I don't know anything about you
and you were right.
But I'm learning.

this microphone only tells the truth
PHILIP WILCOX

this microphone only tells the truth. tomatoes are actually a fruit. men always look better in suits. I don't hate the smell of my own earwax. *this microphone only tells the truth.* seals are really dogs that are mermaids. you have the same number of hours in the day as beyoncé. *this microphone only tells the truth.* the chicken came before the egg. everyone wants roadrunner to be crushed by that anvil. squash are fruit too. god created the world so he could see what his reflection looks like. I mostly like what my reflection looks like but I trust and fear photos more. the average lifespan of a mayfly is a metaphor. the egg came before the chicken. *this microphone only tells the truth.* pumpkins are also fruit. the girl in the front row is kinda cute. I'm gunna assume your name is ruth because it rhymes with. *this microphone only tells the truth.* I'm wearing ill-fitting skinny jeans because I'm insecure about my size. but true beauty is only on the inside. *this microphone only tells the truth.* chillies cucumber capsicum all fruit. fruit bats soar so peacocks don't get too cocky. gen y have the strongest thumbs in human history but the weakest arms. with slam poets moving them like hillsong attendees having a stroke. sharing transcendence like a bottle of coke. giving the illusion of poetic structure while at the same time being the closest thing this white boy will get to being a gangsta rapper. but don't get distracted by these hands. it's this microphone that tells the truth. advising you to tighten your desert tripwires. don't be clueless. don't trust mirrors. remember a mayfly has the same number of hours in the day as beyoncé if beyoncé died halfway during the day. ruth is beautiful. everything is a motherfuckin' fruit. *this microphone only tells the truth*

THIS IS MY MAXIMALIST POEM ABOUT MYSOGYNY
SCOTT WINGS

MYSOGYNY IS SAD
MEN WHO ARE MISOGYNISTS ARE SAD
I HOPE ALL MISOGYNISTIC MEN DIE
SO WE ARE NOT SAD FOR THOSE SAAD MEN

IF THIS WERE A ZOMBIE APOCALYPSE I HOPE ALL THE MISOGYNIST MEN
GET EATEN AND ALL THE GIRLS ARE LEFT HOLDING BLOODY AXES
GORE-SPLATTERD CRICKET BATS SHIRTS RIPPED HALF OPEN BY THE
COUNTLESS ATTEMPTS OF ZOMBIE MEN TO DEVOUR SCANTILY CLAD WOMEN

I COULD BE THE SOLE MALE SURVIVOR

THE ONLY MAN WHO WAS NEVER MISOGYNISTIC

AND WE'D ALL FRESHEN UP AT SOME
SAFE FORTRESS
SOME SHANGRI-LA OASIS
AND ALL THE WOMEN WOULD BE HAVING SHOWERS AND GETTING
INTO PILLOW FIGHTS AND THEN WE'D BE UNDER ATTACK BY A BREACH
OF MISOGYNY ZOMBIES AND THERE'D BE NO TIME TO ZIP UP THEIR JACKETS

OR TIE THEIR PINK KIMONOS AND THE ONLY WAY TO DEFEAT MISOGYNY
ZOMBIES IS TO SHOOT THEM IN THE DICK OR CUT OFF THEIR COCKS WITH
NINJA SWORDS AND MINI SKIRTS AND ALL THE GIRLS WOULD BE LIKE
'GIRL POWER'
AND I'D BE LIKE
'YEAH!'
AND THEY'D EYE ME SUSPICIOUSLY
THEY'D SHOOT ME IN THE DICK IN A SECOND IF I BEGAN TO CHANGE
BUT I'D BE THE ONLY NON-MISOGYNISTIC MAN ON THE PLANET
THE ONLY ONE WITH IMMUNITY TO DICK INFESTATION AND ALL THE GIRLS
WOULD HAVE TO LOOK AFTER ME AND BAKE ME CUPCAKES SO I COULD
REPOPULATE THE WORLD WITH MY RESISTANT STRAIN OF DNA

IF I WAS ON THE BEACH BEING SURROUNDED BY ZOMBIES
ALL THE GIRLS WOULD RUN TO PROTECT ME AND BECAUSE ZOMBIES ARE
TRADITIONALLY SLOW-MOVING CREATURES THEY'D ALL RUN IN SLOW-
MOTION BUT BEING A NON-MISOGYNIST I'D FIND FLOWERS TO GIVE THE
GIRL THAT I LOVED: THE HUGE AMAZONIAN QUEEN WIELDING TWIN
CHAINSAWS AT THE FRONT OF THE BATTLEGROUND
AND ALL THE GIRLS WOULD BE LIKE: 'WHY DO YOU LOVE HER?' AND I'D
SAY, NON-MYSOGYNISTICALLY, THAT SHE'S A REAL WOMAN AND DOESN'T
CONFORM TO BODY STEREOTYPES TOUTED IN THE MEDIA AND THE GIRLS
WOULD SAY, 'THAT STUPID BITCH

HAS STOLEN ALL OUR FOOD SUPPLIES
WE ARE SKINNY COS WE ARE STARRRRVING'

AND THE HUGE AMAZONIAN QUEEN WIELDING THREE CHAINSAWS AT THE
FRONT OF THE BATTLEGROUND WOULD ACCUSE THEM OF LYING AND THEY
WOULD FIGHT AND ROLL AROUND IN THE MUD AND THE DIRT AND THE SAND
AND GET NAKED SOMEHOW THEY GOT NAKED WHILE FIGHTING

BUT BEING A NON-MYSOGYNIST
I'D WALK AWAY
LAMENT ALL THE FALLEN SOLDIERS
WISHING FOR A BETTER DAY

AND THAT'S THE END OF MY POEM ABOUT MISOGYNY

The pigeon is a Big Man
TROY WONG

My therapist wants to know if i was breastfed
I have a short attention span and get bored easily

My Mum yells abuse   at me as i'm leaving
for work   One morning   i move out and live

in Granville   I cover my balcony with plastic grass
Two pigeons make their nest there   green

& purple like oil on wet asphalt   I have
a short attention span   She lays two eggs

behind the milk crates   I hold them in my palm like
coins   I put them back   South Street on Sundays

is a tunnel of chicken smoke   Road rules are optional
Cars smash like eggshells   His red eyes are goji berries

He puffs himself up with popcorn & cigarettes
When i stand up too fast   he vanishes in a puff

of smoke   They gather twigs & shit   everywhere
they stay   Because   it is a Safe Place   i live in

Granville and my barber is probably a drug front
So is that juice place no one ever goes to

At night the stray cats snarl & rip at each other
Making love sounds   a lot like a catfight

I have a short attention span but some things
i remember all the time like   I'm two years old

on the kitchen counter at my parents' house
and my Mum says You know your Daddy & i

love you very much   I'm twenty-three now and
there's so much i don't know   I try to say Love

and say Loud instead   try to say Mum say Mad
instead   try to say Mum say Mouth instead and it

swallows me whole   Family comes out Felony
Safe comes out Scathe   Dad comes out Dead

This pigeon is a Big Man   My Dad is more pigeon
than man   Mum raises her voice and he vanishes

in a puff of smoke   drives a white van around Sydney
gridlock like an egg stuffed between milk crates

She gathers coins for her empty nest   I grow
old and walk around with fists full of twigs

& broken eggshells   I slot my hands in
my pockets like coins   I don't know what to do

with them   I have four parents   Three of them
are pigeons   Two are roosting on my balcony

One is a stray cat   At night i lock my doors &
windows   Some things i can block out but others

i remember all the time like   My first word
was Car   not   Mum or Dad

Box
LUKE WREN REID

I gotta buy a house
I have to have a place to live in
A white walled box to fit my safety in
Some walls and rooms to bury my dreams in
Some job from which to shovel the foundations
In from

You need to buy a house
Something to work for
A comma on the way to
A full stop
Some punctuation of survival
That barricades the useful from the vacant lot

You need a house to live in
A box to bury your dreams in
A casket to prove you died and were forgiven
Proof of your willingness to conform to something
To prove in the afterlife

That you had a house

I live in a structure made from desires
That fence me in
I am an ocean in a bathtub in a rented house with the blinds shut

We cut down the forests of our dreams
Mill the ancient lumber
Nailed like Christ statues in even rows
Hang frozen limbs in dramatic poses

Plumb ... between the joists
String lined to the framework
Below the hallowed beams

I need this house!

This frame to keep me
From suffering the sky completely

We carry our dead to fireplace each night
The television crackles a eulogy
The warmth is expected and the colour drains
The fire cracks whilst the sap spits

We were never meant for this

The homes of our dreams had windows
To let the night breeze in

I gotta get a house!

I need to prove my worth
Is worth the air I have been breathing
Am I stealing every time my lungs are filling?
Am I blowing down houses
With my greed for believing?

The only box I want to be in has colourful wrapping
I want my gifts to be given
I want a house that's a home that my heart can fit in

Everyone is building
So few are living

But you gotta have a house
Because the homeless are dying
When the audits are in
You better have a debt

With a name and address

I get the internet
QUAN YEOMANS

I get the internet
I get the internet
I get it in my home
I get it on my phone
I get it through the air
I get it everywhere

I can touch the universe
Through my tiny screen
I'm a digital extrovert
On the digital scene

I may look like I'm asleep
But I'm piloting my rocket
I got all my friends with me
I keep them in my pocket

When I'm at work, work, work
I make a search, search, search
I've gotta get that Information
And make it hurt, hurt, hurt

Cats
Pornography
Information
I get it

Haters
Trolls
Paedophiles
I don't give a fuck
Whatever

Now I'm living in the wi-fi zone
In outer space but I'm never alone
I'm just trying to make a real connection nection, nection, nection

I get the internet
I get the internet

Collecting data
To feed my start-up
I'm targeting your satisfaction

Sculpting my meta
To make it better
Please rate this interaction

No more decisions
Just algorithms
To take you where you need to be

Want you to be a part of
This conversation
That I've been having with me

I get the internet
I get the internet

Hey, Mary Shelley
EMILIE ZOEY BAKER

Hey, Mary Shelley.
I'd love to time travel into you, go back to 1818
and get inside your body like a flexible ghost.
I'd like to kiss science-electricity astronomy
and chemistry-feminism on the mouth with you.
We'd brush your hair and I'd watch your
cheeks in the mirror being peach.
I'd see you putting on your corsets resentfully.

Then later on we'd fuck your husband,
the renowned poet Percy Shelley.
He'd fuck us with fairy queens in his head,
before zombies were characters,
before vampires had rules,
because
you haven't even invented science fiction yet, Mary Shelley.
You wrote sick wonderful fiction with your tongues
and performed unholy acts, 'cause
nature was your God.
Your glory hole was the entire house.
You made hot blind music
that couldn't live between just four lines or four legs.
Monsters were everywhere in 1818.
Before electricity, candle flames
made demons on the walls like TV,
the underworld was well above ground,
nights would rule and bellow above your lives,
and you can't fight the ghasts of the universe with a candle,
but you were never afraid of the dark, Mary Shelley.
You'd drink dust and remain unaware that leeches
are weird to put on people as a cure.

There's a movie that just came out called *Mary Shelley*, Mary Shelley.
I think you'd hate it – I've seen the trailer.
It's 200 years since *Frankenstein* was published.

I'd like to whisper fragile to you, while I'm living in your body, that it's a
    fine piece of work
and it will make you immortal,
and not to sweat the small stuff.
Like a brain tumour.

So the actor playing your husband,
the tortured, rejected from polite society for his radical views
and brilliant poet, Percy Shelley, is super lame,

like, straight from the set of *Gossip Girl*.

You won't know what that is, Mary Shelley,

but trust me.

His moussed hair is not accurate and
Byron, that sex poet, looks like he dyes his moustache with …
I'm trying to think of something black you might know in 1818 …
Maybe … octopus ink.
He looks like he dyes his moustache with octopus ink.

And it doesn't capture you at all.
The woman who plays you is nothing but your thimble,
her skin is as thin as a day moon.

The film doesn't get it, about the terror of atheism
in the nineteenth century,
fucking with fairy queens in your head,
cold feet, muddy streets
and cheap alcoholic kerosene afternoons.

It doesn't get that having stillborn babies
will make you crazy unless you have something like
poetry to fish out the dead hearts from your own body.

That you were one of the lucky ones –
you made a rope ladder out of words.

Women were blamed for things like that,
told they had Satan in their bellies or some flomp.

Satan was big back then, but not so much anymore.
Satan is only in the mouths of crazy people now.
He's got a lot less sway.

While I'm in your limbs, Mary Shelley,
I'll touch us on the temple and let you know
I am sorry you had to see your mother as a gravestone only.
I can't imagine what it must be like to carry the pain
of her dying in childbirth when you are that child.

Women had no voice, no platform, no therapy,
no way to process that medieval-level trauma.
And the fact she was replaced by a witch with a poisoned-apple mouth
is okay 'cause it set you on your path
and pulled your voice like a ribbon through history.
Mary Shelley, you shook towers for us,
set fires and burned down forests,
you took the nails out so
we could push down the churches of literary patriarchy.

I would like to stay in you until you die,
to write with you, hear Percy tell you,
'Poetry is a mirror which makes beautiful that which is distorted'.
And you, drunk on inkwell fever,
I want to watch you trust yourself in a world that says you can't.
Watch you stand up for your Medusa brain,
too wild for a bonnet.
You wore those corsets upside down,
your thoughts sewn onto your clothes
with the stitches showing.
Not afraid of archaic laws in black wooden rooms,
or propaganda, or Catholics,
not afraid of the darkness.
Not afraid at all.

Realpolitik
MOHSEN SOLTANY ZAND

I see a donkey that is singing for democracy
I see a hyena that is waiting for the 'war on terror'
I see a shark that is helping rescue boat people
I see a prisoner mouse making a party for the cat
I see a fox teaching freedom to the hen and rooster
I see an executioner putting the mask of religion on his face
I see a locust sowing a green field for humanity
I see an elephant stepping tentatively to avoid crushing the ant
I see a hungry wolf shaking hands with a lamb
Pity us because we think these animals are a symbol of humanity's progress
I see people who are blind to all but the magic box
I see people who are deaf to all but the animal's song
I see people who are working for humanity, but with only the power to worry
I saw democracy in the oil
I saw humanity in the bullet
I am obsessed with death, I wait for it like crazy,
Because death is better than the real world.

Notes on contributors

Hani Abdile is based in Sydney Gadigal of the Eora Nation. She spent months in immigration detention where she found healing in writing poetry. Hani is an honorary member of PEN International and lead member of Writing Through Fences. She is the author of *I Will Rise*.

Jessica Alice is a poet, critic, broadcaster and artistic programmer living on Kaurna land in Adelaide. She is the Director of Writers SA, the peak organisation for literature in South Australia. Jessica's writing and reviews have been published in *Guardian Australia*, *Metro* magazine, *Overland*, *VICE*, *The Lifted Brow*, *The Victorian Writer* and *Cordite*.

Eunice Andrada is a Filipina poet, teaching artist and performer. Her debut poetry collection, *Flood Damages*, was shortlisted for the Victorian Premier's Literary Awards (2019). She has performed her poetry on diverse international stages, from the Sydney Opera House to the UN Climate Negotiations in Paris.

Evelyn Araluen is a poet and researcher working with Indigenous literatures. She has won the Nakata Brophy Prize for Young Indigenous Writers, the Judith Wright Poetry Prize, and a Next Chapter Fellowship with the Wheeler Centre. Born, raised and writing on Dharug country, she is a descendant of the Bundjalung nation.

Ken Arkind is a writer and educator living in Aotearoa. A US National Poetry Slam Champion, he has been performing and teaching internationally for almost two decades. He is the author of the poetry collection *Coyotes*, and currently works as a Poet and Youth Development worker for Action Education.

Tusiata Avia was born in Christchurch, where she is a poet, performer and children's book writer. She is the author of *Fale Aitu / Spirit House*, *Bloodclot* and the highly acclaimed *Wild Dogs Under My Skirt*, which she adapted for the stage.

Maryam Azam graduated with Honours in Creative Writing from Western Sydney University and holds a diploma in the Islamic Sciences. She is the recipient of a WestWords Emerging Writers' Fellowship and a member of SWEATSHOP: Western Sydney Literacy Movement. Her debut poetry collection is *The Hijab Files*.

Hinemoana Baker is a New Zealand writer and performer living and working in Berlin. Her stage shows pivot around sonic art, lyric poetry and family storytelling. She was born in Ōtautahi/Christchurch. Hinemoana traces her mixed ancestry from England, Germany and several Māori tribes. She was the 2009 Arts Queensland Poet in Residence.

Courtney Barnett is a songwriter, singer and musician. She is the first female solo artist ever to win ARIA's Best Rock Album. She was nominated for Best New Artist at the 58th Annual Grammy Awards and for International Female Solo Artist at the 2016 Brit Awards.

The Bedroom Philosopher is a thermonuclear song and dance man from Tasmania c/o Melbourne. He has released several albums including the ARIA nominated *Songs from the 86 Tram*. As Justin Heazlewood he has published three books, including a recent childhood memoir.

Hera Lindsay Bird is a writer from Wellington, whose first book was *Hera Lindsay Bird*. Her most recent publication is the chapbook *Pamper Me To Hell & Back*. She likes murder mysteries and watching figure-skating.

Amy Bodossian is a critically acclaimed performer and published poet who has appeared on ABC's *Spicks and Specks* and *Please Like Me*, performed at major festivals across Australia, headlined Melbourne's top poetry events, been nominated for a Green Room Award and won the 2017 Melbourne Spoken Word Convenor's Choice Award.

Behrouz Boochani is a Kurdish-Iranian writer, journalist, scholar, cultural advocate, filmmaker and human rights defender currently incarcerated by the Australian government on Manus Island. His memoir – *No Friend But the Mountains: Writing from Manus Prison* – won the 2019 Victorian Premier's Prize for Literature and for Nonfiction. Boochani also co-directed the documentary *Chauka, Please Tell Us the Time* with Iranian filmmaker Arash Kamali Sarvestani.

C.J. Bowerbird is the 2012 Australian Poetry Slam Champion and a TEDxCanberra performer. He has released *Beyond This Blue*, a recording of the show he created with the Downfall Choir for the 2017 National Folk Festival. He combines words and clumsy movement as part of the Sound & Fury Ensemble.

Allan Boyd (aka the antipoet) is a performance poet based in Perth. Known for his 'difficult and acerbic words', he has been writing, performing and organising poetry and poets since 1995. Allan is the WA coordinator of the Australian Poetry Slam, teaches Experimental Writing at Curtin University and runs Perth Slam.

Jakob Boyd (aka Laundry Man) is a performance poet, events organiser and indie publisher raised in Perth's anarchist community. Boyd has organised a myriad of grassroots events and projects in Perth's poetry and music scenes and has performed in events, festivals and theatre in WA, NSW and Victoria.

Jesse John Brand is an Australian Poetry Slam National Champion, author of *Cranes Falling in Unison*, and the multi-instrumentalist behind the electronic hip hop project Wolves. What a fucking legend.

Ben Brown (Ngāti Pāoa, Ngāti Mahuta, Ngāti Pakeha) has been a writer, poet and pen for hire for nearly thirty years. He is an award-winning children's author, and his poetry has been published and recorded widely throughout New Zealand and around the world. He is also the father of two glorious children, his best work to date.

Eddy Burger is a Melbourne writer of funny and experimental performance poetry and fiction. His work has been published in literary journals, chapbooks and spoken word CDs. He is an anti-realist, literary radical and champion of the imagination – a former winner of the Melbourne Fringe Festival's Spoken Word Award.

Pascalle Burton is a poet and performer with an interest in conceptual art and cultural theory. She is the author of the collection *About the Author Is Dead* (Cordite Books). Other projects include UN/SPOOL (with Nathan Shepherdson), 24 Hour Gym (with Tessa Rose), the zine series *Today, the* *voice you speak with may not be your own*, and performing in the band The Stress of Leisure.

Rhyan Clapham (aka Dobby) is a rapper, drummer, speaker and workshop facilitator. He proudly identifies as a Filipino and Aboriginal musician, whose family is from Brewarrina on Ngemba land, and is a member of the Murrawarri Republic in Weilmoringle, NSW. He is also a skilled composer and was the 2017 recipient of the biennial Peter Sculthorpe Fellowship.

John Clarke (1948–2017) was born in New Zealand. He was and remains one of Australia's best-known and most-loved faces on TV. He was a comedian, writer and actor.

Maxine Beneba Clarke is the ABIA, Indie and multiple Premier's award-winning author of the short fiction collection *Foreign Soil*, the memoir *The Hate Race* and the poetry collection *Carrying the World*. Her acclaimed picture books include *The Patchwork Bike*, *Wide Big World* and *Fashionista*. Poetry is her first love.

Claire G. Coleman is a Wirlomin Noongar woman whose ancestral country is in the south coast of Western Australia. Her debut novel, *Terra Nullius*, was shortlisted for the Stella Prize and an Aurealis Award and won the Norma K. Hemming Award. *The Old Lie* (2019) is her second novel. She also writes essays, short fiction and poetry.

Jennifer Compton lives in Melbourne and is a poet and playwright who also writes prose. When it comes to the poetry side of things she likes to have it every which way possible. She very much likes winning the Newcastle Poetry Prize and being given the big cheque. And she also very much likes the hurly burly of the open mic.

Arielle Cottingham absconded to Australia with one suitcase and her mother's miniature coffee maker in 2015. She won the Australian Poetry Slam in 2016 and published her debut collection, *Black and Ropy*, in 2017. She still travels the world with one suitcase and the coffee maker.

Damian Cowell (behind a mask and pseudonym) was the voice of Aussie rock icons TISM – a collision of music, satire, art and outright offensiveness the likes of which we will never see again. He continues to joyously juggle highbrow and lowbrow with his group Damian Cowell's Disco Machine.

Emily Crocker has performed at events including BAD!SLAM! NO!BISCUIT!, Noted Festival, Storyfest, Sydney Fringe, Wollongong Writers Festival and Word in Hand. She is the author of the chapbook *Girls and Buoyant*. Her poems have also appeared in journals such as *Australian Poetry Journal, Cordite, Southerly* and *Verity La*.

Nathan Curnow is a lifeguard, poet and spoken word performer. His previous books include *The Ghost Poetry Project, RADAR, The Right Wrong Notes* and *The Apocalypse Awards*. In 2018 he toured Europe with singer–songwriter Geoffrey Williams, performing at festivals in Poland and Germany.

Koraly Dimitriadis is the author of *Just Give Me The Pills* and *Love and Fuck Poems*. These poetic works form the basis of her theatre show *KORALY: 'I say the wrong things all the time'*. Koraly is an opinion writer and the recipient of a Wheeler Centre Fellowship. www.koralydimitriadis.com

Tug Dumbly is a poet and satirist who has performed as a radio regular (Triple J, ABC Local Network) and in schools, venues and festivals in Australia and abroad. He has released two spoken word CDs through the ABC and three times won the Nimbin World Performance Poetry Cup. His first collection of poems is *Son Songs*.

Quinn Eades is a research fellow and lecturer at La Trobe University. His poetry collection, *Rallying*, won the 2018 Mary Gilmore Award. Quinn is the author of *all the beginnings: a queer autobiography of the body*, and the co-editor of *Going Postal*, and *Offshoot: Contemporary Life Writing Methodologies and Practice*.

Alice Eather was an Indigenous poet, teacher and environmental activist from Maningrida in the Northern Territory.

Ali Cobby Eckermann's first collection, *little bit long time*, was written while she was living in the desert. In 2013 she won the Kenneth Slessor Prize for Poetry and Book of the Year in the NSW Premier's Awards for *Ruby Moonlight*, a massacre verse novel. In 2014 Ali was the inaugural recipient of the Tungkunungka Pintyanthi Fellowship, and the first Aboriginal Australian writer to attend the International Writing Program at University of Iowa. In 2017 Ali received a Windham Campbell Award for Poetry from Yale University.

David Eggleton lives in Dunedin and was the co-winner of the PEN New Zealand Best First Book of Poems Award in 1987. His collection *The Conch Trumpet* won the 2016 Ockham New Zealand Book Award for Poetry, and he received the 2016 Prime Minister's Award for Literary Achievement in Poetry.

Lorin Elizabeth is a spoken word poet, organiser and teaching artist from Thirroul, who co-founded Enough Said Poetry Slam and is published in *Going Down Swinging*'s audio anthology. In 2018, Lorin featured at Australian Poetry Slam heats with the Queensland Poetry Festival and led workshops and panels for the Stella Prize's Girls Write Up program.

Due to a bewildering series of clerical errors, **Tim Evans** has spoken his words at people in venues all over Melbourne and Victoria, in New York, and at the National Poetry Slam in Chicago. He encourages us to recognise the overwhelming angst of human existence then laugh in its face.

Gabrielle Everall completed her PhD in creative writing at UWA where she wrote her second book of poetry, *Les Belles Lettres*. She has been published in numerous anthologies including *The Penguin Anthology of Australian Poetry*. She has performed at the Bowery and the Edinburgh Fringe.

Bela Farkas is a Canberra-based poet. He has featured at BAD!SLAM! NO!BISCUIT!, Traverse Poetry Slam, West Word Poetry, You Are Here, Noted and as part of the ACT Australian Poetry Slam. His work is published in *Delinquent*, *Otoliths*, *Tundish Review* and *Under Sedation: A Performance Anthology of Canberra Poetry*.

Jayne Fenton Keane has been extensively published in print, radio, digital, performance, sound and visual mediums. She has published three books, *Torn*, *Ophelia's Codpiece* and *The Transparent Lung*, and is currently working on a new poetry manuscript with support from Arts Queensland.

A Murri man, born on Wakka Wakka land at Barambah, now known as Cherbourg Aboriginal Reserve near Murgon, Queensland, **Lionel**

Fogarty has been involved in Aboriginal activism from his teenage years on issues such as Land Rights, Aboriginal health, and particularly deaths in custody, following the death of his brother, Daniel Yock, in 1993. He is an award-winning Australian poet who has published fourteen collections since 1980.

Benjamin Frater (1979–2007) considered his poetry part of a tradition that included Spenser, Milton, Blake and Ginsberg. Though he never completed his University of Wollongong degree, he became, near enough, its poet-in-residence. Suffering from schizophrenia he refused to let it impede his creativity and friendships.

Zenobia Frost is a poet based in Brisbane. She received a 2018 Queensland Literary Fellowship and won the 2018 Val Vallis Prize for 'Reality on Demand'. She watches a lot of renovation TV for 'poetry reasons'.

Bjork once said 'you shouldn't let poets lie to you', but **Fury** writes poetry, which is a sort of lie, albeit the fun-for-everyone kind. Fury has written a book called *I Don't Understand How Emotions Work*. It is very good book; soft and tricky, like leaning your face against your favourite swan.

Andrew Galan masterminded the ACT poetry slam: BAD!SLAM! NO!BISCUIT! He has featured nationally and internationally, and his poetry appears in the *Best Australian Poems, Nuovi Argomenti, The Canberra Times, Cordite* and more. His collection, *For All the Veronicas (The Dog Who Staid)*, won a 2017 ACT Writing and Publishing Award.

Ian Gibbins is a widely published poet, video artist and electronic musician with four collections of poetry, all in collaboration with artists. His video and audio work has featured in gallery exhibitions, public art commissions, performances and international festivals. He was previously a neuroscientist and professor of anatomy.

Anahera Gildea (Ngāti Raukawa-ki-te-tonga) is an essayist, poet and short story writer. Her work has appeared in multiple journals and anthologies, and *Poroporoaki to the Lord my God*. She is currently undertaking doctoral research focusing on Māori literature at Victoria University of Wellington in Aotearoa.

Maddie Godfrey is a Perth-bred writer and educator. They have performed poetry at the Sydney Opera House, Royal Albert Hall, St Paul's Cathedral and Glastonbury Festival. Maddie's work aims to facilitate compassionate conversations about social issues. Their debut collection, *How To Be Held*, is a manifesto to tenderness.

Hadley is a crime writer, poet and bookseller from Canberra/Brisbane/Sydney. He has performed his work at the Cloncurry Merry Muster and Rodeo, Sydney Opera House, Queensland Poetry Festival and Northern Territory Writers Festival, where a leather daddy nearly choked him to death with a fistful of pavlova.

David Hallett has been taking his poetry from the page to the stage since the mid-1970s. He is the host of two of Australia's longest-running spoken word venues in Byron Bay and Lismore.

Jordan Hamel is a Wellington-based poet and public servant. He grew up on a diet of Catholicism and masculine emotional repression. He's the 2018 New Zealand Poetry Slam Champion. He has performed across Aotearoa. He wants to publish a book, so a tangible piece of his vanity will outlive him.

Mohamed Hassan is a poet born in Cairo and raised in Auckland. He is the 2015 New Zealand Poetry Slam Champion, a TEDx fellow and represented New Zealand at the Individual World Poetry Slam in 2016. He is the author of the poetry collection, *A Felling Of Things*.

Kelly Lee Hickey was raised on the sweat-soaked wetlands outside of Darwin and continues to live and work in the Northern Territory, on Arrernte and Larrakia land. An Australian Poetry Slam Champion, her work has been published and performed in Australia, China, Finland, New Zealand, Indonesia and Germany.

Dominic Hoey is an author, playwright and poet based in Auckland. He has performed his poetry around the world. His debut novel, *Iceland*, was a NZ bestseller and longlisted for the 2018 Ockham Book Awards. His recent one-person show was nominated for Outstanding new New Zealand Play of the Year at the 2018 Wellington Theatre Awards.

Eleanor Jackson is a Filipino–Australian poet, performer, arts producer and community radio broadcaster. She is the author of *A Leaving*, and her live album, *One Night Wonders*, is produced by *Going Down Swinging*.

Joelistics's great gift is the crafting of common language into evocative turns of phrase. As a rapper, songwriter, multi-instrumentalist, producer, actor and advocate for diversity, he is recognised as a unique voice in the Australian music scene, from his early seminal work with alt-rap group TZU, to working as a solo artist, to the critically acclaimed theatre show *In Between Two*.

Teri Louise Kelly is the author of three memoirs and one poetry collection. She was featured in the ABC radio documentary *The Poet Stripped Bare* and was the subject of the DVD *TLK Punk*. She has appeared at numerous spoken word events nationally and internationally.

Zohab Zee Khan is a motivational speaker and multidisciplinary artist. He was the 2014 Australian Poetry Slam Champion and is the co-founder of the Pakistan Poetry Slam. Over the last ten years he has conducted more than a thousand poetry and self-development workshops across the globe.

Simon Kindt is a poet, performance artist and teacher from Brisbane. His work explores the intersections of language, sound and performance.

Laniyuk was born of a French mother and a Larrakia, Kungarrakan and Gurindji father. She was a contributor to the anthology *Colouring the Rainbow: Blak Queer and Trans Perspectives*, as well as the winner of the Indigenous residency at Canberra's Noted Writers Festival in 2017 and *Overland*'s Writers Residency for 2018.

Klare Lanson is a poet/writer/artist, whose collaborative performance projects explore social failure and place-making. She was co-editor of *Going Down Swinging*. Recent projects include *#wanderingcloud*, *Commute*, and mobile art ethnography *TouchOn/TouchOff*. Klare is a PhD candidate at RMIT University and co-editor of *The Routledge Companion to Mobile Media Art*.

Daisy Lavea-Timo is an orator, rugby league prop and producer. Her poetry explores what it means to be a straddler of worlds as a kiwi-born, fluent-Samoan speaking and traditional tattoo-wielding Matai/chief. Crowned the 2017 NZ Slam Poetry Champion, Daisy is currently Southern Regional Manager for the Ministry of Youth Development.

Michelle Law is a writer working across film, theatre and print. Her work includes the hit play *Single Asian Female*, and the SBS web series *Homecoming Queens*, which she co-created, co-wrote and starred in.

Luka Lesson is a poet and rap artist of Greek heritage who has toured extensively in Australia and abroad over the past eight years. He is the author of two collections of poetry and two albums, and was the 2010 Australian Poetry Slam Champion and the 2011 Melbourne Poetry Slam Champion. In 2018 he was commissioned by the QSO to write a concerto named *Macquarie*, and has collaborated on *Odysseus*, a live re-imagining of Homer's *The Odyssey*.

L-FRESH The LION is a hip hop artist from south-west Sydney. From the same mould as J. Cole and Black Thought from The Roots, his music is grounded in thought-provoking lyricism, providing social commentary from the perspective of an Australian born to migrant parents from Punjab, India.

Eleanor Malbon has performed poetry in festivals and events throughout Australia, including the You Are Here festival and Crack Theatre festival. Her poems have been published nationally by *Cordite*, Grapple Publishing, Express Media and internationally by New River Press. She writes new words for ecological crisis and the age of endings.

Sara Mansour is a lawyer, spoken word artist, and co-founder and director of Bankstown Poetry Slam, Australia's largest regular poetry slam. Sara has been recognised through a number of awards for her leadership. This is the first time Sara's work is being published, and she is 'so excited, omg'.

Selina Tusitala Marsh (ONZM) is New Zealand Poet Laureate (2017–19) and takes poetry to a wide range of people and places, from primary schoolers and presidents, to corporates and the Queen. She lives in the hope that maybe one day one of her rugby-league-lovin' sons will write her a poem.

Laurie May is the Artistic and Festival Director for the Red Dirt Poetry Festival and The Dirty Word. In 2012 she won the Central Australia Poetry Slam. Laurie May lives in Alice Springs where she is a mentor and workshop facilitator in remote communities of the Northern Territory.

Ian McBryde is a Canadian-born Australian poet. He has published ten books of poems and three audio CDs of spoken word poetry and original music.

Laura Jean McKay is the author of *Holiday in Cambodia* and *The Animals in That Country* (forthcoming). She is a doctor of fiction with a PhD from the University of Melbourne. She lectures in creative writing.

Courtney Sina Meredith is a poet, playwright, fiction writer and musician. Her publications include the play *Rushing Dolls*, poetry collection *Brown Girls in Bright Red Lipstick* and short story collection *Tail of the Taniwha*. Her poetry and prose have been translated into Italian, German, Dutch, French, Spanish and Bahasa Indonesia.

Performing writer **Miles Merrill** brought poetry slams to Australia from Chicago. His work is the catalyst for most spoken word projects in Australia. Merrill directs the literary organisation Word Travels and is founder of the international Australian Poetry Slam. He publishes text, video and audio but is best live.

Misbah (Wolf) is an acclaimed Pakistani-Australian poet. Poems from her collection, *Rooftops in Karachi*, have previously appeared in *Mascara Literary Review, Cordite, Contemporary Asian Australian Poets* and *Peril*.

Scott-Patrick Mitchell is a West Australian performance poet and writer who appears in *Island, Southerly, Westerly, Cordite* and *Rabbit*. In 2015 SPM performed the one-person show *The 24 Hour Performance Poem*. Currently he is exploring concepts of ritual, magic and healing in his performance poetry.

Morganics is a Cairns-based award-winning hip hop artist, spoken word performer, director and community worker. NB No hipsters were harmed in the making of his song.

Wiradjuri and Gamilaroi **Lorna Munro** is a dynamic artist–educator working with visual arts, spoken word poetry, experimental performance art, radio, film, television, theatre and set design. She calls the Redfern–Waterloo Gadigal country home. Lorna has featured at the Sydney Writers' Festival, Adelaide's Spirit Festival, Boomerang Festival and Yabun Festival.

Djapu woman, mother, wife and writer **Melanie Mununggurr-Williams** writes about being all these things. She writes about autism and how it affects her family, and about love. Melanie hopes that doing what she loves with passion, she will encourage youth, especially girls, to do the same.

Omar Musa is a Malaysian–Australian rapper, novelist and poet from Queanbeyan, Australia. He is a former winner of the Australian Poetry Slam and the Indian Ocean Poetry Slam. He is the author of the novel *Here Come the Dogs* and two poetry books (*Parang* and *Millefiori*), and has released three hip hop albums including *Since Ali Died*, which has now been turned into a one-man play.

Anisa Nandaula is the 2016 Queensland Poetry Slam Champion, the runner-up Australian Poetry Slam Champion and a nationally renowned poet. She is an Arts Queensland XYZ 'Innovation in Spoken Word' recipient, has published a collection of poetry, and performed her work at the Queensland Poetry Festival, Townsville Multicultural Festival and the Sydney Opera House.

Ngā Hinepūkōrero is a spoken word group comprised of four wahine who are all students of Ngā Puna o Waiorea, in Auckland. Their spoken word journey resulted in their winning both the 2018 WTFL Youth Slam and the Trans-Tasman Slam.

Steven Oliver is a sexy poet. Not that he writes sexy poetry, rather that he is sexy simply when being a poet onstage. He is a poet influenced by his Kuku Yalanji, Waanyi, Gangalidda, Woopaburra, Bundjalung and Biripi heritage, which makes him even waaaay sexier.

Jesse Oliver is a Perth-based performer, writer and Australian Poetry Slam Champion. He has featured internationally and also at the Byron

Bay Writers Festival and TEDxPerth. On stage, Jesse delivers a unique conversational style, highlighting the power of vulnerability as he explores homelessness, mental illness and gender.

Sean O'Callaghan is Irish of a sort, the sort who didn't think he belonged there so left like so many Irish writers before him, to be here, which is not there but getting there in many ways, and his writing somewhat reflects this.

Angela Peita is a spoken word artist, youth and community worker, workshop facilitator and live art producer. She is co-founder and co-director of Ruckus Slam, the hugely popular Brisbane slam and arts company.

Kiri Piahana-Wong is a New Zealander of Māori (Ngāti Ranginui), Chinese and Pākehā (English) ancestry. She is a poet and editor, and is the publisher at Anahera Press.

ΠΟ. was born in Greece in 1951, came to Australia in 1954 and grew up in Fitzroy. *Big Numbers* collects his new and selected poems, while *Fitzroy – The Biography* is his latest work of poetry. He has represented Australia at many festivals including the 1997 International Poetry Festival in Colombia and the 2003 Weltklang Festival in Berlin. He is currently editor of the experimental magazine *Unusual Work*.

Te Kahu Rolleston is a writer, activist, battle rap artist, actor, and scholar and educator of legal rights, NZ History, Te Reo Maori, and many other things. He uses his skills and passions for words as a way to educate and firmly believes that: 'if you are to speak, you had better say something worth hearing.' *Tauranga Moana Tauranga Tangata*.

Tessa Rose is a poet and performer. She has been published in *Cordite* and in *Today, the voice you speak with may not be your own* (Lavender Room), and has performed her work at the Queensland Poetry Festival, COUPLET, Woodford Folk Festival, Noted Festival and other venues across Australia.

Candy Royalle (1981–2018) was an award-winning writer, performance artist, poet and activist well-known to audiences in Australia and around the world. Sadly, Candy passed away in June 2018 from ovarian cancer.

Her poetry, essays and opinion pieces continue to be published widely. She is remembered by her family and the LGBTQIA+ community for her strength, conviction and passion.

Max Ryan is lead singer and lyricist with the band Hexham. His first book, *Rainswayed Night*, won the Anne Elder Award for poetry.

Omar Sakr is an Arab–Australian poet. His debut collection, *These Wild Houses*, was shortlisted for the Judith Wright Calanthe Award and the Kenneth Slessor Prize. His new book is *The Lost Arabs*.

Sara Saleh is an Arab-Australian poet and long-time campaigner for refugee rights and racial justice. Sara's first poetry collection was released in 2016, and her poems have been published in English and Arabic in several publications. Sara is co-curator of *Growing Up Arab-Australian* and working on her debut novel.

Ben Salter is a songwriter and performer from Australia. He has been active as a recording artist and performer since 1995, both solo and as a member of a wide variety of ensembles including Giants of Science, The Gin Club, The Wilson Pickers, The Young Liberals. He has toured extensively throughout Australia and across the globe.

Ray Shipley is a comedian, performance poet and librarian. Ray has won the Christchurch Poetry Slam three times and placed third nationally in 2018. Their debut comedy show, *He & She*, was nominated for Best Newcomer at the New Zealand International Comedy Festival, also in 2018.

Steve Smart is a poet and performer based in Footscray, Victoria. Lately he spends most of his time organising and hosting events around Melbourne, but he's looking forward to getting back to the quill and ink in 2019. He tends to write in hectic bursts anyway.

Amanda Stewart is a Sydney-based poet, author, producer and vocal artist. She has created a diverse range of publications and has performed solo and in collaborative ensembles throughout Australia, Europe, Japan and the US, working in literature, new music, broadcasting, sound poetry, theatre, film and new media environments.

Grace Taylor, of Samoan, English, Japanese heritage, was born in Aotearoa. She is a mother, poet, theatre maker and has two published works, *Afakasi Speaks* and *Full Broken Bloom*. She wrote the Auckland Theatre Company show *My Own Darling*, and was the recipient of a CNZ Emerging Pacific Artist Award (2014) and International Writer-In-Residence at the University of Hawaii Manoa (2018).

Sandra Thibodeaux is a poet and playwright. She has published four collections of poetry, the most recent being *DIRTY H20*. In 2011 Sandra was Australian Poetry's Poet-in-Residence. Sandra has written over a dozen plays that have been staged as part of festivals in Indonesia and Australia, receiving nominations for the Patrick White, Griffin and Green Room Awards.

Tayi Tibble (Te Whānau-ā-Apanui/Ngāti Porou) is a writer, editor and Indigenous arts administrator from Te Whanganui a Tara. Her first collection of poetry is *Poūkahanagtus*.

Merlynn Tong is an actor and playwright. She is adapting Sophocles' *Antigone* for Queensland Theatre Company's 2019 season. Her plays *Ma Ma Ma Mad* and *Blue Bones* are published by Playlab. In 2018, *Blue Bones* won six Matilda Awards, including the Lord Mayor's Award for Best New Australian Work.

Saba Vasefi is a multi-award-winning journalist and academic. She writes for the *Guardian* on the narratives of displacement, researches her PhD on Exilic Feminist Cinema and teaches at Macquarie University. Her poems have appeared in a variety of journals including *Transnational Literature* and *Wasafiri Magazine of International Contemporary Writing*.

Samuel Wagan Watson is a state and national multi-award-winning poet and professional narrator and storyteller who has Irish, German, Dutch and Aboriginal (Munaldjali and Birri Gubba) ancestry. In 2018 Samuel was awarded the prestigious Patrick White Literary Award. He is the author of three chapbooks and five collections of poetry.

Taika Waititi is a New Zealand film director, screenwriter, actor and comedian. His feature films include *Boy, Hunt for the Wilderpeople, What We*

Do in the Shadows co-directed with Jemaine Clement, and *Thor: Ragnarok*. **Emily Beautrais** is the Creative Director at Clemenger BBDO Wellington.

Ania Walwicz has published six books: *Writing, Boat, Red Roses, Elegant, Palace of Culture* and *Horse*. Her work has been included in over 200 anthologies. Spoken word performances of her work feature in live events, theatre, films, sound recordings and on YouTube.

wāni is a Congolese trans-disciplinary artist from Walungu, currently based in Naarm (Melbourne). He often speaks in third person and addresses himself as the last afronaut. More often than not he doesn't really feel like he belongs to this planet. But as of right now, he is alive and doing just fine.

Jahra 'Rager' Wasasala is of Fijian/Euro origin based in Aotearoa and an award-winning cross-disciplinary artist and world-builder. Her work has toured internationally, including to Australia, Hawaii, New York, Berlin, Guåhån and Canada. In 2016 Jahra received the Prime Minister's Pacific Youth Award for the Arts.

Teila Watson (aka Ancestress) is a Birri Gubba and Kungalu/Gungalu Murri, and a multitalented artist and writer. Known for her political and provocative style of addressing world issues, Teila's practice revolves around climate change, ecological and social sustainability, and therefore importance of Land Rights and First Nations Sovereignty.

Indigenous writer, poet and storyteller, **Uncle Herb Wharton** received the Australia Council Award for Lifetime Achievement in Literature, an award that recognises eminent writers who have made outstanding and lifelong contributions to Australian literature.

Sean M. Whelan is a poet, playwright, DJ, marriage celebrant and podcaster. He has published two books of poetry, *Love is the New Hate* and *Tattooing the Surface of the Moon*. In 2018 he began a weekly creative-writing-themed podcast called *More Than a Whelan*.

Philip Wilcox is a full-time teaching and touring poet. He is a former Australian Poetry Slam Champion and two-time New South Wales Poetry Slam Champion. His first collection is *Beetle Prayer*.

Scott Wings is a performance artist, spoken word artist, physical theatre practitioner and event host based in Melbourne. He is the curator and director of a range of immersive, interactive and community performance with Ruckus Melbourne. Scott currently lectures in drama at Melbourne University's Trinity College.

Troy Wong was born and raised in Western Sydney. He helmed both Parramatta Poetry Slam and Granville Poetry Slam as host and creative director and was a national finalist in the 2015 Australian Poetry Slam. Troy's work has been featured in *Australian Poetry Journal, Cordite* and more.

Luke Wren Reid is a Tasmanian writer and photographer. He is a two-time Australian National Poetry Slam finalist, a featured poet at the Tasmanian Poetry Festival, and was accepted to the Banff Spoken Word Residency in Banff, Canada. Luke continues to write and perform in his home state, Tasmania.

Almost half a century ago, without much warning, **Quan Yeomans** was yanked out of his mother's warm insides with a pair of cold, steel forceps. He understandably began screaming and has not stopped since.

Emilie Zoey Baker is an award-winning poet, teacher and spoken word performer who has toured internationally. She was a fellow at the State Library of Victoria, coordinator of the Australian National Slam, and was core faculty for the spoken word program at Canada's Banff Centre.

Iranian poet **Mohsen Soltany Zand** arrived in 1999 from Iran and was held in Australian immigration detention for four years. His work is published in a variety of journals and anthologies, produced as recordings, and in the book *Inside Out*. His performance of *Australian Dream* premiered at the Queensland Poetry Festival in 2017.

Acknowledgements

Poems from this collection have appeared in the following books and magazines, some of them as earlier versions:

Jessica Alice's 'Landmarks' appeared in *Australian Poetry Journal 8.2 – 'Spoken'*, from australianpoetry.org, 2018.

Eunice Andrada's '(Because I am a daughter) of diaspora' appeared in *Flood Damages*, Giramondo, 2018.

Evelyn Araluen's 'Fern your own gully' appeared in *The Lifted Brow*, Issue 40 – *Blak Brow*, 2018.

Ken Arkind's 'Godbox' appeared in *Coyotes*, Penmanship Books, 2014.

Tusiata Avia's 'Three reasons for sleeping with a white man' appeared in *Wild Dogs Under My Skirt*, Victoria University Press, 2004.

Maryam Azam's 'A brief guide to hijab fashion' appeared in *The Big Black Thing: Chapter 1*, ed. Michael Mohammed Ahmad & Winnie Dunn, Sweatshop, 2017; and *The Hijab Files*, Giramondo, 2018.

Hinemoana Baker's 'If I had to sing' was commissioned by Christchurch Art Gallery Te Puna o Waiwhetū on the occasion of the Gallery's reopening in December 2015 after five years of closure following the Canterbury earthquakes of 2010 and 2011.

Courtney Barnett's 'Depreston' appeared on the album *Sometimes I Sit and Think, Sometimes I Just Sit*, 2015.

The Bedroom Philosopher's 'In my day (Nan)' appeared on the album *Songs From The 86 Tram*, Nan & Pop Records, 2010.

Hera Lindsay Bird's 'Children are the orgasm of the world' appeared in *Hera Lindsay Bird*, Victoria University Press, 2016.

Behrouz Boochani's 'Forgive me my love' appeared in Richard Mosse's *The Castle*, Mack, 2018.

Jakob Boyd's 'Employment separation certificate' appeared in *City Without Stories*, Indifference Publications, 2018.

Ben Brown's 'Moko' appeared in *Between the Kindling and the Blaze*, Anahera Press, 2013.

Eddy Burger's 'My VICES' appeared in *Beinart, Angel Circus, Humans, animals & objects*, 2007, *Overland* online and *Voiceprints 10* CD, F...loose Productions, 2010.

John Clarke's 'Sigrid Sassoon: The Prime Minister' appeared in *The Even More Complete Book of Australian Verse*, Text, 2012.

Maxine Beneba Clarke's 'gil scott-heron is on parole' appeared in *Carrying the World*, Hachette, 2016.

Jennifer Compton's 'Love is not love' appeared in *Barefoot*, Picaro Press, 2010.

Arielle Cottingham's 'Tramlines' appeared in *Black and Ropy*, Pitt St Poetry, 2017.

Emily Crocker's 'Spooks' was first published in *Cordite Poetry Review*, 2018.

Nathan Curnow's 'Corpse fete' appeared in *The Apocalypse Awards*, Australian Scholarly Publishing, 2016.

Koraly Dimitriadis's 'My wedding dress' is an excerpt from the poem 'Best Friend' and appeared in *Love and Fuck Poems*, Outside The Box Press, 2012; and *Audio Overland II: Resistance*, ed. Maxine Beneba Clarke, from overland.org.au, 2013.

Tug Dumbly's 'My country' appeared in *Son Songs*, Flying Island Books, 2018.

Quinn Eades's 'What it's really like to grow up with lesbians in the 70s and 80s' appeared in *Australian Poetry Journal 8.2* – 'Spoken', from australianpoetry.org, 2018.

Alice Eather's 'Yúya karrabúra (Fire is burning)' appeared in *Growing Up Aboriginal in Australia*, ed. Anita Heiss, Black Inc, 2018.

Ali Cobby Eckermann's 'Circles & Squares' first appeared in *little bit long time*, Australian Poetry Centre New Poets series, 2009.

David Eggleton's 'Taranaki bitter' appeared in *Catalyst* and *Time of the Icebergs*, Otago University Press, 2010.

Lorin Elizabeth's 'Leaves' appeared in *Eat Read 'Zine* Lorin Elizabeth & Laurie May.

Tim Evans's 'Poem, interrupted' appeared in *Australian Poetry Journal 8.2* – 'Spoken', from australianpoetry.org, 2018.

Gabrielle Everall's 'Vita means life' was inspired by *The Letters of Vita Sackville-West to Virginia Woolf*, ed. Louise DeSalvo and Mitchell Leaska, Hutchinson and Co, 1984; and appeared in *Going Down Swinging* and *Les Belles Lettres*, General Chaos Press, 2017.

Bela Farkas's 'Brushing with Tom' appeared in *The Tundish Review*, Issue 6.

Lionel Fogarty's 'SCENIC MAPS PARTS' appeared in *Eelahroo (Long Ago) Nyah (Looking) Möbö-Möbö (Future)*, Vagabond Press, 2014.

Benjamin Frater's 'To kill the Prime Minister' appeared in *6am in the Universe*, Grand Parade Poets, 2011.

Zenobia Frost's 'Reality on-demand' appeared in *Cordite Poetry Review*, 2018.

Fury's 'when they legalise gay marriage' appeared in *Going Down Swinging* and *Going Postal*, Brow Books, 2018.

Andrew Galan's 'Art, industry, architecture & pets' appeared in *Today,* *the voice you speak with may not be your own*, from thevoiceyouspeakwith. wordpress.com; *For All the Veronicas (The Dog Who Staid)*, Bareknuckle Books, 2016; and appeared with audio-visuals by _f_k at Queensland Poetry Festival, 2014.

Ian Gibbins's 'dog daze' is a video poem and appeared on vimeo. com/238368813.

Anahera Gildea's 'Sedition – a letter to the writer from Meri Mangakāhia' appeared in *Poetry*, Poetry Foundation, from poetryfoundation.org, 2018.

Maddie Godfrey's 'Labels are for jars' appeared in *Voicemail Poems* and *How To Be Held*, Burning Eye Books, 2018.

Jordan Hamel's 'Ham and cheese toasties' appeared on *EYEGUM*, from www.eyegum.org.

Mohamed Hassan's 'Customs: a love story' appeared on *The Wireless*, from radionz.co.nz/news/the-wireless.

Kelly Lee Hickey's 'How to stay afloat' appeared on *The Disappearing*, Red Room Poetry, from disappearing.com.au.

Eleanor Jackson's 'When women go to war' appeared in *Shave and a Haircut*, self-published by Betsy Turcot & Eleanor Jackson, 2014.

Joelistics' 'Nostromo' appeared on the album *Blue Volume*, 2014.

Teri Louise Kelly's 'Girls like me' appeared in *Girls Like Me*, Wakefield Press, 2010.

Klare Lanson's '#commute' is a collaboration with composer/musician Damian Mason developed through the Undue Noise Collective, and a 2014 Punctum Inc Live Art Seedpod residency. It appeared as a mobile media art film in QPF's O<PEN> project, 2015; and a mobile art ethnograph entitled TouchOn/Touch Off, 2017.

Daisy Lavea-Timo's 'Whakamana' appeared at *TEDx Christchurch*, from tedxchristchurch.com/daisy-lavea-timo, 2018.

Michelle Law's 'The wheel' appeared in *Brisbane Poetry Map*, Queensland Poetry Festival, 2015.

Luka Lesson's 'Yiayia' appeared in *The Future Ancients*, from www.lukalesson.com.au, 2013.

L-FRESH The LION's 'The LION Speaks' appeared on the album *The LION Speaks*, 2012.

Eleanor Malbon's 'Somehow fragile' appeared on *Feminartsy*, from feminartsy.com, 2015.

Sara Mansour's 'My Australia' appeared in *Where Poetry Thrives*, The Sydney Culture Essays, from sydneycultureessays.org.au, 2017.

Selina Tusitala Marsh's 'Pussy cat' appeared in *Tightrope*, Auckland University Press, 2017.

Ian McBryde's 'Spree' appeared in *Equatorial*, Five Island Press, 2001, and *We the Mapless: New and Selected Poems*, Barenuckle Books, 2017.

Courtney Sina Meredith's 'No motorbikes, no golf' appeared in *Brown Girls in Bright Red Lipstick*, Beatnik Publishing, 2012.

Miles Merrill's 'Night's knows' appeared in *The Penguin Anthology of Australian Poetry*, ed. John Kinsella, Penguin, 2009; and on the album *What Night Knows*, 2003.

Misbah's 'Rooftops in Karachi' appeared in *Mascara Literary Review*, from mascarareview.com; and *Rooftops in Karachi*, Vagabond Press, 2018.

Morganics's 'Hipster killer' appeared on the album *For My Friends and My Enemies*, 2016.

Omar Musa's 'The boys' appeared in *Millefiori*, Pengiun, 2017.

Anisa Nandaula's 'Human' appeared in *Melanin Garden*, Clark and Mackay, 2018; and appeared at *TEDx Brisbane*, 2017.

Angela Peita's 'Ways to draw blood from feathers' appeared in *Pressure Gauge Journal*.

Kiri Piahana-Wong's 'Of books and bookcases' appeared in *Dear Heart: 150 New Zealand Love Poems*, ed. Paula Green, Godwit, 2012; and *Night Swimming*, Anahera Press, 2013.

Π.O.'s 'Memo' appeared in *925 Magazine*, 1983; and *BIG NUMBERS: new and selected poems*, Collective Effort Press, 2008.

Candy Royalle's 'Impermanent' appeared in *A Trillion Tiny Awakenings*, UWA Publishing, 2018.

Max Ryan's 'Old guys' appeared in *Australian Poetry Journal 8.2 – 'Spoken'*, from australianpoetry.org, 2018.

Omar Sakr's 'How to live in a world that is burning' appeared in *Verity La*, from verityla.com, 2017.

Sara Saleh's 'InshaAllah' appeared in *Australian Poetry Journal 8.2 – 'Spoken'*, from australianpoetry.org, 2018.

Ben Salter's 'No security blues' appeared on the album *The Stars My Destination*, 2015.

Amanda Stewart's 'postiche' appeared in *I/T: Selected poems 1980–1996*, Here and There Books, 1998.

Grace Taylor's 'Tinā (Mother)' is a video poem comprised of three poems; 'Storm of a Woman' appeared in *Full Broken Bloom*, Ala Press, 2017, and 'Tinā I & II' appeared in *Afakasi Speaks*, Ala Press, 2013.

Sandra Thibodeaux's 'An early survey of principles' appeared in *Dirty H20*, Mulla Mulla Press, 2014.

Tayi Tibble's 'Assimilation' appeared in *The Spinoff*, from thespinoff.co.nz, 2018; and *Poukahangatus*, Victoria University Press, 2018.

Samuel Wagan Watson's 'When pencils sing excuses' appeared in *Love Poems and Death Threats*, University of Queensland Press, 2014.

Taika Waititi & **Emily Beautrais**'s 'Give nothing' marked the launch of the ongoing nationwide *Give Nothing to Racism* campaign developed by the New Zealand Human Rights Commission Te Kāhui Tika Tangata, and Clemenger BBDO Wellington. The campaign encouraged the public, and leaders across business, the education sector, cities and councils, sports organisations and more to address racism in New Zealand.

Ania Walwicz's 'doctor proctor' appeared on Andrée Greenwell's album *Listen to Me*, 2018; and appeared in *Australian Poetry Journal 8.2 – 'Spoken'*, from australianpoetry.org, 2018.

Sean M. Whelan's 'You probably think this poem is about you (and it probably is)' appeared in *Tattooing the Surface of the Moon*, Small Change Press, 2008.

Troy Wong's 'The pigeon is a Big Man' appeared in *Cordite Poetry Review*, 2017.

Quan Yeomans's 'I get the internet' appeared on Regurgitator's album *Headroxx*, 2018.

Emilie Zoey Baker's 'Hey, Mary Shelley' appeared in *Australian Poetry Journal 8.2 – 'Spoken'*, from australianpoetry.org, 2018.

Mohsen Soltany Zand's 'Realpolitik' appeared on the album *Australian Dream*, 2005; in *Southerly*; and in *Inside Out*, Kardoorair, 2010.

Tapu tapu te korero / **Remember the sacredness of the spoken word**

We both acknowledge and pay our respect to the Bundjalung nation on whose land we did most of the editorial work for *Solid Air*.

We are deeply grateful to the families of artists who are no longer living, for their support in having their loved one's work featured in *Solid Air*. Sincere thanks to the families of John Clarke, Alice Eather, Benjamin Frater and Candy Royalle. We encourage you to read their pieces out loud to keep their voices alive, to keep their words burning bright.

We are indebted to all the poets who have contributed to this groundbreaking collection. Without your work we are nothing but hot air.

Huge thanks to Des Skordilis for the inspired poetic *Solid Air* artwork and her exceptional interpretation skillz.

There is no *Solid Air* without the generous funding from the Australia Council of the Arts and Creative New Zealand Toi Aotcaroa. These two peak arts bodies saw our vision and we are thankful for their financial support.

Many thanks to the University of Queensland Press for backing this project, opening the poetry door a little wider.

We thank the magnificent and badass Alison Whittaker for writing such a stunning Foreword. Buy her *Blakwork* (Magabala Books, 2018) now.

Ngā mihi maioha ki a houtou